Book Cover by Raylee Gunter

First Edition 2024

ISBN: 978-1-963985-02-3

Journey of the Bride

Volume II

Seasons

*There is a season (a time appointed) for everything
and a time for every delight and event or purpose under
heaven—A time to be born and a time to die; A time to
plant and a time to uproot what is planted. A time to kill
and a time to heal; A time to tear down and a time to build
up. A time to weep and a time to laugh; A time to mourn
and a time to dance. A time to throw away stones and a
time to gather stones; A time to embrace and a time to
refrain from embracing. A time to search and a time to
give up as lost; A time to keep and a time to throw away.
A time to [a]tear apart and a time to sew together; A time to
keep silent and a time to speak. A time to love and a time to
hate; A time for war and a time for peace.*
Ecclesiastes 3:1-8 Amp

Dedication

This is a dedication to the remnant bride of Christ. Hold fast my beloved brethren to what you have, that no one may take your crown. I charge you to keep your lamp burning, as your love for your savior remains kindled and strong. Let Him find you in faith upon His return.

In persecution remember, God sees you. You shall remain clutched in His arms of grace and protection. Run the race to win for you have an imperishable crown awaiting. Let your faith remain a burning inferno, as you finish the race of salvation with victory. Do not be led astray by false doctrine. Instead, be diligent in studying His word and show yourself approved as you continue to discern and rightly divide the word in excellence. Remain relevant, uncompromisable, and blameless in the purity of His word.

Stay spiritually rich so when He comes, He will not find you bankrupt, naked and poor. For remember a crown of His glory awaits all those who faint not. Be faithful in your pursuit. Persevere, for your bridegroom gave a promise. He will write a new name upon you, as He makes you a pillar in the temple of His God. Hold fast! Be not part of the world, remain distinctive set apart, for you are mine.

Remember you are promised to me, therefore remain faithful for you are betrothed. Your bridegroom is on His way. Keep your lamp lit with oil. Have a reserve and fall not asleep. Watch and pray as you remain diligent in anticipation of my arrival, for I Am draws nigh. Be found clothed in readiness.

Love Abba-Father

Note From the Illustrator

Hello! My name is Raylee, and I'm 15 years old! The author asked me to design the cover of this book. I've already created the cover of the first book in this series, and I wanted to share my inspirations and experiences while designing the second book! When the author told me the book's title, Seasons, I immediately thought, "Oh, like the seasons Winter, Summer, Fall, Spring." I thought about it a bit more and also remembered how Ecclesiastes talked about different seasons and timing in our lives. I didn't really know how I would recreate that on a book cover until God gave me a beautiful image in my head of a single tree representing all the different seasons. The tree, with its changing leaves and weathered bark, symbolizes the passage of time and the different stages of life. I started working on it, and before I knew it, I had the image that was in my head on paper. I think the tree is a great analogy for how one tree (one person) can go through many seasons in life. Changing physically, emotionally, mentally, and most importantly, spiritually.

Testimonial

As one of the editors, I offer the following disclaimer for the trigger warning you may encounter as I share my testimony of the journey taken while editing the book "Seasons." Words fail to capture the turmoil I experienced upon starting this project. Despite having worked on Volume 1 of this series, this book was different; it challenged me deeply, flooding my mind with questions like: Who am I and why? And the even more profound question: Who did God create me to be? The inner conflict was intense because these two questions seemed irreconcilable. The editing process took much longer than I had anticipated. To continue effectively, I had to absorb, reflect on, and contemplate the profound statements and questions within the content.

A video of my life began to play right before my eyes as memories rushed in, taking my breath and stripping me of control. Nothing remained hidden. Every hurt, pain, betrayal, abuse, and bruise replayed in my mind. Anger surfaced as my perception of life and expectations began to unravel. I was furious that I couldn't trust the people around me to keep me safe, especially since sexual abuse had started at a very young age. Anorexia and bulimia became my coping mechanisms, but the anger within only grew. Becoming pregnant at sixteen and marrying an alcoholic and drug addict added more fuel to my inner rage. Rape, betrayal, divorce, and various forms of abuse shaped a version of me clouded by anger. This anger distorted my self-image, causing me to see myself in a way that was far from God's intention.

My heart had become hardened by life's trials making it difficult for me to grasp God's grace. Yet, in a pivotal moment, His mercy washed away my confusion, and His grace enveloped me. Through the lens of the Holy Spirit, I began to see things in a new light. The aha moment came when I realized that the person, I was most angry with was myself. I questioned why I had made certain choices and why I hadn't recognized my own worth. My heart, bruised, cut, and scarred over time, had only received superficial treatment. I applied pressure to stop the bleeding but never gave the wounds the care they needed for true healing. This insight marked a significant turning point in my journey towards healing.

My motto of "all is well" was no longer sufficient. The questions I faced were meant to uncover the hidden pain from my childhood through adulthood. I tried to evade and dismiss them, but I couldn't. A response was necessary before I could move forward; I couldn't keep editing my life. As emotions surfaced, I was overwhelmed with grief for the care I had given my younger self. I was stopped in my tracks, tears flowing and causing me to pause everything.

But these tears were not in vain. I encountered the One who makes all things possible—the God of Hope. The truth began to flow freely: I had spent much of my life editing myself to meet my own and others' expectations, growing frustrated when things didn't align with my plans. At that moment, I experienced a profound self-realization. I had been living a life of self-editing, trying to fit into others' molds. Now, I was ready to embrace the truth, release the anger and self-deception, and surrender to God's plan for my life. This moment of transformation and surrender inspired and motivated me to move forward.

I no longer needed to pretend to be someone I wasn't. All my defense mechanisms were exposed truth came to light. The different seasons of life began the necessary work to shape me into who God intended me to be. I realized this was essential for my growth. At that moment, surrender became crucial. I had to decide if I was willing to let go of everything and embrace God's plan for my life, including releasing my pride. God knew exactly when to dismantle the barriers and "do not enter" signs in my heart. His transformative power pierced through, revealing and uprooting everything didn't align with His promise. As I waited for Him to bring balance to every emotion and thought within my soul, I found encouragement and peace. Turning my heart back to God and recommitting my life to Him, I acknowledged that His ways and thoughts are far beyond my own.

So much has been dismantled, and the process of rebuilding is underway. My delicate state is being perfectly aligned with His plan. As we move in harmony, I find myself affirming, "Yes, Lord, your ways are best." My spirit finds joy and contentment in this journey. The goodness of God is undeniable. His love has dispelled all my fears and confirmed His unwavering faithfulness as a Father who will never abandon me.

My faith in God has been a guiding light, filling me with hope for what's to come. Jeremiah 29:11 resonates deeply with me: "For I know the plans I have for you," declares the LORD, "plans to prosper you and not to harm you, plans to give you a hope and a future." I recognize that I wouldn't be who God created me to be—made in His image—without His transformative power.

Humble servant of the Lord,

Lorraine Hughes

Seasons of the Soul

Introducing the newest gems in the Lord's treasure chest:

The precious gems I've unearthed in my spiritual journey have not only deepened my relationship with the Lord but also sparked a sense of curiosity and wonder. They have led me to pause and bask in His presence, shutting out the world to hear His whisper.

Rest, I found, was the most challenging aspect of my journey, demanding a stillness I wasn't accustomed to. I used to see stillness as a waste of time amidst my many tasks, revealing my inner Martha while my soul's Mary urged me to sit at the Master's feet. This was my aha moment – an intentional choice to surrender and spend time with the Lord.

Embracing **Selah,** I found the rest needed and a renewed hunger for His presence, where clarity and peace became my guide.

Journaling has become vital to this journey, turning my inner thoughts into written dialogue with God. Once afraid to put to paper what is in the confines of the heart and mind, I experienced a newfound freedom. As the Lord answered and guided me through my petitions, I found inspiration and courage in the act of journaling.

Rest:
Rely in me so I might **E**mpower you by my Spirit as you **S**urrender all that hinders you to total **T**rust in your Father. Let me finish the work needed to equip you properly for the task before you. ***Love Abba-Father***

Selah Moments:
Define Selah: Tranquil, secure at rest. Silence, quiet, peaceful serene. A time to pause and ponder the truth that has been said or sung.
Quiet your soul as you learn to pause, ponder, bask and rest in His presence.

Journaling:
Grab a book and writing tool. I find a multi pens works best for me, for I can write in one color and go back and read it and underline with another color, oftentimes finding certain words jump out at me! Don't stop to try to figure it out, let the pen flow. The time for understanding comes later. Through this process our relationship with our Heavenly Father is built. Trust is firmly established as our eyes are enlightened to the possibilities of all that the Lord can and so desires to do for us.

One must **REST** before they can embrace the **Selah moments** to prepare the heart to **journal**!

Table of Contents

Prologue

Prologue

Ecclesiastes 3:1 There is a season (a time appointed) for everything and a time for every delight and event or purpose under heaven.

In the tapestry of life, there are many seasons that weave together a story. Seasons of joy and sorrow are made evident as I walk the path marked out for me. God's plan is like a diamond, with many facets displaying all the necessary seasons. And like a diamond the cuts are what brings forth brilliance and allows the light to reflect in multiple directions all at once. We are that diamond!

So I often ask, "***What season am I in***?" For every season is necessary to bring us to the very image we were created to be. We have been given a precious gift – time! But time marches on ***Tick Tock***. With each passing moment, choices are required.

In the valley of decision, the hardness of heart must be broken down. With great patience and perseverance, the ***tilling of the soil*** begins. Breaking through the hardness of fear and doubt as fertile ground buried deep within is exposed. I am made ready to receive! He has called me out of the grave, to rise up out of the ashes of despair and adversity.

Through all the trials and tribulations, sorrows and setbacks, I am challenged to emerge stronger than before, as the ashes are a reminder of all that God has burned away.

As the Lord sweeps away all that does not belong, I can now embrace the *ashes to beauty* that reflect the inner workings of the Lord.

My ashes to beauty display the steadfast love of my God and therefore I choose to surrender myself as He leads me to a place where I can *let go and let God* take care of everything, no matter what the season.

With an open heart and a willing spirit, I can relinquish control and trust that *with God all things are possible.* In the letting go I find a peace that surpasses my understanding for this journey of faith assures me of *His great love*.

Embracing His grace, I am able to find strength to overcome every obstacle and the courage to face every challenge. His grace is sufficient. With outstretched arms His unconditional love has poured forth in overflowing measure assuring me that I am His and He is mine.

Chapter 1 What Season Are You In

There is a season (a time appointed) for everything and a time for every delight and event or purpose under heaven Eccl 3:1

These words resonate within my heart as the new chapter of my life unfolds, my appointed time and purpose for the revelation of God's plan to be disclosed. In my self-discovery, I will attempt to embark on the wisdom that the Lord unveiled to me through scripture and introspection. In the peeling away and with his divine guidance and truth, I will try to unravel the layers of the false identity I once encountered. His love and revelation set me free, so I can now see what was always beneath.

The uncovering has begun—the truth of my Creator's original intended design for me as his creation. Our dialogue now begins as I invite you to explore with me once again a new gem from God's treasure chest.

I hope this gem shines brilliance in your heart and unfolds the truth of who you were always meant to be in Him. It is time for birthing as we embrace the true potential that our loving savior placed within us. May we learn to surrender to God's divine timing, clarity, and purpose so our heart's transformation may begin. Learning to hunger and thirst after divine truth brings spiritual clarity and unveils our spiritual eyes to see more profoundly than what was shown. It is time, my beloved readers, for the exploration to begin; the moment is at hand to align with God's perfect will.

Our Heavenly Father's intentional design is woven into the tapestry of purpose—the golden thread into the very fabric of our existence. My readers, we are not mere afterthoughts; we are purposefully designed vessels with a Heavenly plan. Only in His purpose can we enter into fulfillment of inner peace. For our creator is the open door. May we desire to trust our lives to Him, for that is the best decision we could ever make. Awareness and understanding are a gift from our Father that allows us to walk effectively in our call and purpose of God concerning us as our passion for Him grows.

Selah Moment:

What are you passionate about?

Does it bring you closer to your Savior?

How are you perceiving the seasons of your life?

Are you in tune with God's Divine timing?

Are you ready for your Divine Purpose to be unveiled?

Are you ready to embrace who he created you to be?

Before we can tackle these questions, we must first establish an understanding and clarity of our calling. Otherwise, we cannot effectively walk in the purpose connected to our call. I am finally starting to understand that passion for him cannot be fabricated; it must become the essence of our nature. It must ooze from our being.

Definition of clarity: [Webster dictionary] the quality of being easily seen through, a lack of marks, spots, or blemishes, the quality of being easily understood, the state of having a full, detailed, and orderly mental grasp of something.

Definition of calling: [Webster dictionary] a strong urge toward a particular way of life or career, a vocation. Strong inner impulse accompanied by conviction of divine influence.

Definition of purpose: [Webster dictionary] the reason for which something is done or created or for which something exists.

Definition of passion: [Webster dictionary] A strong liking or desire for or devotion to some activity, object or concept. Intense, driving or overpowering feeling or emotion.

A truth written in John 14:6 Declares Christ is the way, truth and life. This, my readers, is the golden thread woven in the tapestry of our lives, marked out in the beginning of time. As we begin to explore these concepts, I invite you to the transformative power of personal revelation. As I share insight through the illumination of my path by the prompting of the Holy Spirit, my Heavenly Father and I engage in dialogue in our secret place, the place of true communion, the destination of my true purpose unveiled.

Our true purpose can be discovered and born forth only in dialogue with our Heavenly Father. You need to know him to know you. Genesis 1:27 tells us we are created in His image. It's best to converse with the one who knows us best. Would you agree?

Though the issues of life's trials may obscure our vision, God is ever-present in the beauty, amidst the chaos. As we embark on the discovery of our true adversary; our internal self, the false narrative constructed from our distorted perception and clouded vision, the hindrance of purpose, let us not forget the beauty of this journey. Let us peel the layers of deception together. Let us discover the truth of our God-given identity- forged in the image of Christ. Are you ready to confront the lie that plagued your mind and heart? Join me as we journey to unravel what once hindered us and embrace the fullness of life that awaits us; the promise of our God.

This chapter serves as a tantalizing, thought-provoking appetizer for going deeper with your Heavenly Father. It is my prayer that it sparks a hunger in you that propels a deeper understanding of your identity in Christ and His promise.

Define appetizer: something that stimulates a desire for more

Matthew 5:6 Blessed [joyful, nourished by God's goodness] are those who hunger and thirst for righteousness [those who actively seek right standing with God], for they will be [completely] satisfied.

What is righteousness? Right living, right standing with God. In its deeper spiritual meaning, righteousness is the quality of being right in the eyes of God, including character [nature], conscience [attitude], conduct [action], and command [word]. Righteousness is, therefore, based upon God's standard because He is the ultimate lawgiver.

As I attempt to draw parallels to the changing seasons in the scriptures of Eccl.3:1-8, walk with me through the pages as we unravel the birthing process.

Introspection in these verses helps us explore how each phase of life has its unique beauty, purpose, and significance. We position ourselves as we learn to embrace the ebb and flow of life's seasons and find meaning and fulfillment in each moment, the good and evil.

For those unfamiliar with giving birth in the initial stage, persistent contractions cause pain, pressure, and unseen internal stretching in the birth canal. As someone who has undergone this journey twice, I am familiar with the emotional and physical challenges that it brings, from back pain to labor-induced contractions. In saying all that, a picture is

5

forming. The season of birthing, which I find myself in, is accompanied by pain and travailing. A process necessary for God's purpose to birth forth.

Romans 8:29 For those whom He foreknew [and loved and chose beforehand], He also predestined to be conformed to the image of His Son [and ultimately share in His complete sanctification], so that He would be the firstborn [the most beloved and honored] among many believers.

Just as labor pains are portions of the birthing process, so too is the discovery of purpose. The trials in our lives are the tools in the hands of the Father, maneuvering the assurance of us giving birth to His desired end.

James 1:2-4 says: Consider it nothing but joy, my brothers and sisters, whenever you fall into various trials. [3] Be assured that the testing of your faith [through experience] produces endurance [leading to spiritual maturity, and inner peace]. [4] And let endurance have its perfect result and do a thorough work, so that you may be perfect and completely developed [in your faith], lacking in nothing.

A rich passage in God's word teaches us how to count it all joy when we go through all kinds of trials, for they are a tool in the Father's hand that maneuvers our contractions during the birthing process. It is said in this passage how we are to endure the trials and the importance of having a consistent faith in God. By allowing the trials to teach us rather than break us, we learn to obey God's word, put it into action, and no longer be found in just the observance of his word.

Learning to understand timing and how God makes everything beautiful in His proper time, the more profound questions begin to haunt my mind and heart. I can no longer stay surfaced as the stripping of the ideas of my false self and my persona begin to crack. The mask came off, and my willingness to peel away the layers as God revealed the honesty of my true state revealed; the understanding came in that moment.

When everything appears to be falling apart, it is actually falling into place, and it is the time for transformation. Perspective is the key. I saw it crumbling and falling apart, but God saw it coming together. He saw alignment taking place as the formation of His beauty was being formed. Despite the storms of life, we are never alone. Our greatest adversary often lies within us, crafting a false reality and comfort that veers us away from God's truth. We become deceived and our vision distorted, leading us astray. It's time to discard these misleading thoughts and acknowledge our greatest obstacle, which is often ourselves.

Instead of blaming the external forces around us, our upbringing, our issues, and our traumas, we shall desire to shatter the often-flawed mindset, for only in God's truth is clarity gained.

My close friend Lorraine once said, "Perception is a deception that needs correction." Let's consider this statement both literally and spiritually.

Definition of perception: [Webster Dictionary] ability to see, hear or become aware of something through senses. State of being, the process of becoming aware.

Spiritual Definition of Perception: The ability to see beneath the outward form to the underlying often hidden reality.

Definition of Deception: [Webster Dictionary] the act of causing someone to accept as true or valid what is false or invalid, error, inaccuracy of something other than the original design.

Spiritual Definition of Deception: The result of not following or obeying the word of God. A believer that practices doctrines or thoughts contrary to God's word is in danger of being in deception.

Definition of Correction: [Webster Dictionary] 1. The action or an instance of correcting. 2. A change that makes something right. To make or set right: amend. Correct an error or inaccuracy.

Spiritual Definition of Correction: To set right or make straight. To bring to the standard of truth.

The version of self has been amended. We have created an adaptation, a false truth contrary to originally spoken. Until we accept that truth and receive it as our true self, true identity to become what God originally intended cannot be born.

Definition of stronghold: [Webster Dictionary] a place that has been fortified so as to protect against attack. A place where particular cause or belief is strongly defended or upheld.

Selah Moment:

Are you able to discern the strongholds in your life that hinder you in walking in your divine purpose?
What do you see?
What is your belief system?
What lies have you fortified in your mind that caused the false reality which prevents you to grow to become all that God your Heavenly Father and creator intended you to be when he created you?

In life's journey, we have willingly embraced the false narrative that has imprisoned us. This hindrance to our freedom has become the ultimate deception related to our identity theft. My beloved, it is time to become unveiled and let the truth be revealed: God's reflection of what He designed for you and me.

Embracing His truth brings forth the liberation needed. Let us discard, therefore, those cloudy lenses distorting our vision. Let us desire to reclaim our true identity, covered, masked, and imprisoned by trauma, hurts, and pains shackling us from being free. Before judgment arises, beloved, I, too, willingly acknowledge my role in allowing my own identity theft. Our creator intends to be known by you and me so that we may better understand ourselves through His eyes born out of His great love for his creation. It is time to realign; it is time to embrace His love. The Father's greatest pleasure is seeing His creation fulfill their purpose and destiny.

In our pursuit of true transformation, we strayed from the original course, altering ourselves; the blueprint has been lost. Only in rediscovering our Heavenly Father's intent will we be able to choose correctly as we relinquish control and allow His divine kindness to guide us back to the truth to become whole. The original blueprint is the image of God. Without proper correction, this truth can never be seen, let alone embraced.

As we embark on a journey of rediscovery, we shed layers of falsehoods, and our authentic selves emerge. My dear readers, this courageous step to giving birth is the liberation designed by our creator. He delivers true fulfillment to us through His divine purpose. We will learn to trust in our Heavenly Father with all our hearts as we lean no longer to our understanding, learning to acknowledge Him in all our ways as He makes our path straight (Proverbs 3:5-6)

Consider this tantalizing morsel on your taste bud at this very moment as we commence on a sumptuous feast ahead and embark on this expedition together in the seasons to come. Let this introduction whet your appetite for the deeper revelation in the coming chapters. May the morsels given activate your hunger for his truth, stirring your heart to desire authenticity and propelling you to seek truth as we journey together in transformation.

My readers, we are at the appointed time. It is the Lord's delight for you to know the purpose under Heaven concerning you; are you ready to be rediscovered?

Dialogue with God:

My child, you are in the new season. Shall you choose to trust me even when you cannot see? Even in the storms of life, your Father shelters you. When you are at your weakest, it is my strength that propels you to not give up, for your creator is here.

I am always in your midst. Find strength in my presence, my child. Please keep your eyes on me and faint not, for a beautiful story is being formed. Push, let the birthing bring forth. My grace is made sufficient in your weakness. Surrender your doubts, your thoughts, and your fears. Let my love in, for it is a love like no other. Let it free you in your innermost being, for all shall work together for your good, you'll see. It is your Savior leading you. Will you trust? Will you believe it? Will you allow me to lead? Let Faith rise!

Selah Moment:

As you journey with the artist, listening to the lyrics below, allow the songs to minister to your heart and connect you with the still, small voice amid the chaos. Grab your journal and jot down what the Lord impresses upon your heart as you listen, engaging in this adventure by faith. Expect to hear Him speak, and with an open heart, you will.

Whatever your plan is by Josie Buchanan/moments
Every Season by Canyon Hills worship
God of New Seasons by Naomi Akuchie Cantwell, Gustavo Antonio- Christ for the Nations.

Personal Reflections:

Chapter 2 Tick Tock

Time to be born and a time to die Eccl 3:2

I am in the season of dying to self to be born again to the creative purpose of God and His original design and intent. It's time to be born again. Incorruptible seed of the word of God. A time to be born to his truth. A time to recognize and acknowledge his way is best. It's the only way that truly makes sense. You have surrendered your thoughts and accepted the truth of his word with your whole heart.

Isaiah 55:8-9 "For my thoughts are not your thoughts, Nor are your ways My ways," declares the Lord. "For as the heavens are higher than the earth, so are My ways higher than your ways and My thoughts than your thoughts."

Reading the scripture mentioned above, we understand that God's infinite wisdom and power have no limits. We can embrace the truth that He alone is God, and we will never fully understand Him, His ways, or His greatness. This clarity frees you and me as we surrender to it; we stop trying to make ourselves this new us. We accept what He has purposed, what He has already created, and walk in that intent. All pressure is off of us, see! It's already been done. Stop trying to be what you think you are supposed to be and just be who He says you already are. This epiphany connects to Repentance.

The biblical definition of Repentance is the act of leaving what God has prohibited and returning to what He has commanded. To change mind, heart, and action by turning away from sin and self and returning to God.

An event in which an individual attains a divinely provided new understanding of their behavior and feels compelled to change that behavior and begin a new relationship with God

Definition of Command: dominate a strategic position from a superior height. To give an authoritative order.

When we, His children, accept that we are His children and did not create ourselves, but He is our creator. We can tackle the disinformation in our minds and eradicate those thoughts that displaced our identity in the first place. Okay, are you ready to tackle this passage of His word with me? I hope you like roller coaster rides. Put on your seatbelt and sit tight. It might get a little bumpy. I hope you didn't eat a big lunch. Hold on, here we go!

A time to be born and a time to die. Hmm, what does that mean? Looking back over my life and assessing through God's lenses some decisions I've made, good and bad, I have come to embrace the truth of God's sovereignty and mercy. Where there's a beginning of a thing, there's also an end. But in all that occurs, my assurance lies in the ultimate authority, which is that God is in control of all aspects concerning me.

He is not at all surprised by the decisions that I have made or will make. In life, there is always a process. There is an appointed time in God's elaborate scheme of destiny concerning my life. He alone decides the length of our days. My life, your life, is in His hands.

Birth is a profound mystery and miracle that comes from God almighty alone. We all have undergone physical birth, which is why you and I are here now. But did you know it didn't stop there? A spiritual birth is also necessary to experience His divine light, divine call, and divine purpose in us.

John 1:12 But to as many as did receive and welcome Him, He gave the right [the authority, the privilege] to become children of God, that is, to those who believe in (adhere to, trust in, and rely on) His name

To honestly know Him, you must undergo this birthing. Yours and my identity is in the revelation and acceptance of Jesus Christ, the word of God. By faith, receiving His truth brings forth the new birth, and life in Christ begins.

This new journey in His kingdom perfects His word as He comes alive in you. Life in Him now is being perfected. You are born of the flesh, which is the natural birth. Now, you are born again of the spirit man, the part of you that was once dead. This is the spiritual birth.

When this portion of you becomes alive, you must willingly surrender the old self to this truth to walk as the new person, for God's word is uncontested. Ezekiel 18:4 tells us the soul who sins shall die, and Romans 6:23 confirms this, stating that the wages of sin is death, but the gift of God is eternal life for those who believe.

I was once dead in my sins and transgressions. I didn't know my Heavenly Father. I was in darkness, blinded by the lust of my heart, drunken by the world, intoxicated and hungering for more. My life was in a downward spiral, leading to destruction. The more I dove into sin, the more miserable and hopeless I became. I didn't see a purpose in my life, let alone understand destiny or divine call. I lived for me, myself and I and do you want to know something? That was the most miserable time of my existence. I tried to fill a void in myself with the world's pleasures, which led me always to desire more, never content, never happy.

I didn't understand why. I knew of God. You see, I was not wholly ignorant of the knowledge of the creator, the divine perfect being who created all things. But knowing Him, I did not see how this perfect, holy, divine being, wanted to know me. For in my fictitious self, I was not worth the thought. He was too important, too busy to have time for little old me. I wore fear as a pearl chain, and every decision I made was laced with that mindset.

I couldn't believe his perfect will for my life. Because of the most straightforward truth denied, I didn't know who I truly was; I believed the lie, believed in the hopelessness I felt and not the hope he desired to be for me. I now can give thanks. God allows the struggles to come my way to place a halt to my plans. In my circumstance of unpreparedness, my Heavenly Father revealed Himself to me. In the miracle placed within my womb, His identity suddenly became real to me. I cried out to Him, I asked Him for His help, and you know what? This big God, who holds all that exists in His hands, made time to listen to little insignificant me. The words of death once spoken over my life no longer held me captive. At that moment, my life shattered as His truth came in like a flood.

I am significant, not deserted or rejected. I am desired and loved. The veil was removed as His truth was embraced; His love for me does not depend on my performance. It's not conditional like the only love I knew. This love is unquestionable. I did not merit it; I did nothing to deserve it. He loved me first before I knew or accepted Him; He loved me because God is love. His truth shattered the distorted lens I looked through. I am not limited based on my ideology of self, and neither are you. God's very essence is love. Being born to His truth was the "Born Again" experience needed to begin our journey together. I was set free once I received and accepted the gift of His grace—His love demonstrated by dying on the cross for my sins and paying my debt. I no longer needed to strive for the love that didn't satisfy me, a love that was met with conditions. His love was free. It had no conditions, no expectations of performance. All I needed to do was believe and receive.

Selah Moment:

Are you ready to surrender your heart to Him?
The uninhabited portions?
The empty feeling within you can't shake or ignore?
The hole within you that you try to fill with everything else but him?
Are you ready to lean on Him?

When I acknowledged that my purpose of being created was to worship my Heavenly Father and that my very existence was not by accident or that I was not an afterthought, please make no mistake, my perception began to shift. Don't get it twisted; this newfound truth didn't make me holy or perfect, but it gave me the desire to want to be delivered. I am still working on being perfected in Him. The difference is I am no longer striving to become in my ability. I choose, by faith, with strength and the help of the Holy Spirit, the great counselor who leads me to all truth. We will talk about Him later. I just wanted to make the introduction to encourage you now so you can understand you are not alone. Once you are born of the spirit, you have a helper who will aid and guide you and teach and comfort you. Who, in the end, brings to the light your purpose?

P ut
U nder
R ight
P ressure
O riginal
S tate
E xposed

This revelation accepted came with many challenges. It wasn't easy. For this new life, being born of the Spirit means something needed to die in the flesh; I couldn't have it both ways. Now, I know some of us think it's okay to live in both, but I'm talking about God's divine purpose and destiny. I'm talking about understanding the truth of God's original design, which He proposed when He had you in mind. I couldn't do what I used to; I couldn't continue to fill my heart, mind, or soul with the intoxication of the world. It was time for me to empty myself of all falsehood to be authenticated to become the real. By Faith, I believed and accepted that I was made anew.

2 Corinthians 5:17 Therefore if anyone is in Christ [that is, grafted in, joined to Him by Faith in Him as Savior], he is a new creature [reborn and renewed by the Holy Spirit]; the old things [the previous moral and spiritual condition] have passed away. Behold, new things have come [because spiritual awakening brings a new life].

I had to pour out myself. What does that look like? Well, let's see. If I embrace that He loves me, I now refuse to be trapped by the insincere love I once accepted. The more I knew Him, the more I began to know the real me. The one spoken about in His word. Psalm 139:12-14 is becoming my reality.

Psalm 139:12-14 Even the darkness is not dark to You and conceals nothing from You, But the night shines as bright as the day; Darkness and light are alike to You. For You formed my innermost parts; You knit me [together] in my mother's womb. I will give thanks and praise to You, for I am fearfully and wonderfully made; Wonderful are Your works, And my soul knows it very well.

If you empty a full glass of polluted water halfway and pour purified water into it, is it good enough to drink, or is it still polluted? My thoughts, mindset, and belief system had to come to subjection to His truth. The whole glass of water had to be purified to be filled by Him to be drinkable.

Isaiah 44:3 Amplified version says: For I will pour out water on him who is thirsty. And streams on the dry ground; I will pour out My Spirit on your offspring and my blessing on your descendants;

John 3:5 Jesus answered, Verily, verily, I say unto thee, except a man be born of water and of the Spirit he cannot enter into the kingdom of God.

Where in His remarkable declarations does it read mistakenly to you? Nowhere! Even in my darkest state of being in my thoughts, which were contrary to

His truth, I was formed beautifully and wonderfully. My belief stayed the same as what He originally said. How I feel about myself, see, or believe can never erase the spoken word. Acceptance of this truth is required to be truly free.

Unfortunately, a lot of times, it's easier to accept misinformation than to take what is true. Why? We are persuaded that what others have said about us is fact and that His truth is a lie. In turn, we never reach the potential originally intended. See, without God's word of promise, our identity is projected by the reality we have created.

John 6:63 It is the Spirit who gives life; the flesh conveys no benefit [it is of no account]. The words I have spoken to you are Spirit and life [providing eternal life].

Are you willing to be born of the Spirit through the acceptance of his son Jesus Christ so that your Heavenly Father can bring the birthing of the new? If yes, then you need to understand that God loves you, and His desire is for you to have peace and eternal life.

John 17:3 Now this is eternal life: that they may know You, the only true [supreme and sovereign] God, and [in the same manner know] Jesus [as the] Christ whom You have sent.

Now, let's get down to the nitty-gritty. Most of the time, we exist and do not live. We are victims of our own chaos. Some leave this life without knowing their purpose, potential, destiny, or call. But if you are reading this book in this season of your life, today is the day of salvation and revelational truth. It is not by chance that we are having this conversation now.

The God of Heaven and Earth knew you, knows you. You are not an oversight; you are deliberate and have a purpose. He has fashioned you. You are uniquely designed and made beautiful as you are. There is no need to alter; you are beautiful and loved as you are. Accept this truth into your heart today and be born again, born of His Spirit, His divine nature. Ask Him to come into your heart. Ask Him to reveal Himself to you, and He will.

Repent of your self-reliance. Ask Him to forgive you for leading your life your way. Tell Him you no longer want to lead. Ask Him to come into your heart and make it His home.

Romans 10:9 because if you acknowledge and confess with your mouth that Jesus is Lord [recognizing His power, authority, and majesty as God], and believe in your heart that God raised Him from the dead, you will be saved.

Surrender to His will and experience the miraculous workings of His divine power. If you do this with sincerity, I promise you will not be disappointed. He is God! He is alive, and He awaits to commune with His beloved creation.

*Ephesians 3:17-19 so that Christ may dwell in your hearts through your Faith. And may you, having been [deeply] rooted and [securely] grounded in love, **18** be fully capable of comprehending with all the saints (God's people) the width and length and height and depth of His love [fully experiencing that amazing, endless love]; **19** and [that you may come] to know [practically, through personal experience] the love of Christ which far surpasses [mere] knowledge [without experience], that you may be filled up [throughout your being] to all the fullness of God [so that you may have the richest experience of God's presence in your lives, completely filled and flooded with God Himself].*

Did you feel the tugging, the pulling? Can you dismiss this gnawing feeling that cannot be shaken? Something bigger than yourself has been trying to get your attention. Do not be afraid or skeptical; God is real. It is His Spirit that draws. Today, as you read these words on the pages, they are becoming alive in you. Today is the day of salvation, so do not harden your heart.

If you have encountered, embraced, and received, walk this new path and begin this new journey with Him. Connect yourself with a believing church community that teaches the infallible word of God, which will help you grow deeper in your walk with Him, for the incorruptible word tells us so.

Luke 15:10 In the same way, I tell you, there is joy in the presence of the angels of God over one sinner who repents [that is, changes his inner self—his old way of thinking, regrets past sins, lives his life in a way that proves repentance; and seeks God's purpose for his life].

You and I transgressed against God our creator and Father's holy law. The penalty for that is death, but He didn't leave it as it should have been. He came and paid the debt for us because we couldn't pay it. He took the punishment upon himself and died in our place so we may be given new life. Our God is always with us. In the chaos of life and confusion of our thoughts, He is Sovereign now and forever more. His grace is made available and sufficient for us in our weakness.

This decision will revolutionize you to the core of your being. Let this hope become your reality. Let the tugging and wrestling bring forth the surrender of your broken heart. You've done it your way for too long. Like Frank Sinatra's famous words sung at the end of his life. He still had some regrets as he faced the final curtain because he did it his way.

It's time for the new song to spring forth. It's time to dance to a different beat. Today is the day, for tomorrow is not promised. Choose this day; choose life.

Psalm 40:3 He put a new song in my mouth, a song of praise to our God; Many will see and fear [with great reverence] And will trust confidently in the Lord.

Choose the only one that can save. There is none but Jesus Christ. He is the way, the truth, and life. John 14:6 No one comes to the Father except through him.

My expectation began in that encounter. Only my Heavenly Father could create newness of heart. Only He can transform my life and give me purpose and destiny. I found abundant life in Him; I was not living apart from Him. I was existing and failing terribly.

There is a song I used to sing a long time ago. Hillsong United called, None but Jesus! Yes, He was Crucified to set you free. Now you live in this born-again new life to bring him ultimate praise. Listen to it. I pray it will do your soul well and minister to your heart as it did mine.

Selah Moment:

What is this that our Father has for us?

Who do you know that would willingly lay down their life, and die to take the penalty of your wrong upon themselves?

He is calling you; shall you refuse?

Shall He become your hope and delight?

Will you make room for Him in your heart?

If you are at this phase in your life and can relate to what I'm saying, then you understand what you are truly missing and are ready to embrace His love, truth, and divine nature with your whole heart.

Hebrews 11:6-8 Amplified version says: But without Faith it is impossible to [walk with God and] please Him, for whoever comes [near] to God must [necessarily] believe that God exists and that He rewards those who [earnestly and diligently] seek Him. By Faith [with confidence in God and His word] Noah, being warned by God about events not yet seen, in reverence prepared an ark for the salvation of his family. By this [act of obedience] he condemned the world and became an heir of the righteousness which comes by Faith. By faith Abraham, when he was called [by God], obeyed by going to a place which he was to receive as an inheritance; and he went, not knowing where he was going.

Have Faith to believe; have Faith to receive. This cannot be intellectually received; you must believe in Faith with a genuine persuasion of His divine presence. His promise is if you earnestly seek Him, you will find Him.

Definition of earnestly: sincere and intense conviction, not lightly casually serious manner

Faith is the invitation that opens the door to come to our Heavenly Father to trust in Him for our salvation.

Ephesians 2:8-9. For it is by grace [God's remarkable compassion and favor drawing you to Christ] that you have been saved [actually delivered from judgment and given eternal life] through Faith. And this [salvation] is not of yourselves [not through your own effort], but it is the [undeserved, gracious] gift of God; not as a result of [your] works [nor your attempts to keep the Law], so that no one will [be able to] boast or take credit in any way [for his salvation].

For we know in Hebrews 11:1, He tells us that Faith is the confidence, which in Greek means foundation. So, what does that mean? Faith is the only foundation you can build upon between you and God. You and I must have an unshakeable conviction of that hope. The hope of what? I'm glad you asked.

Hope in him.
Hope of his love.
Hope of his faithfulness.

Hope of the assurance we hold fast to, His word and promises towards us. It becomes our evidence and proof of His divine nature. Without Faith, this task cannot be accomplished or obtained. Life in God is by Faith. You cannot receive if you do not believe. Now, Let's uncover the two hindrances of Faith that were once in my life: doubt and unbelief.

The biblical definition of doubt: to call into question the truth wavering to feel uncertain lack of conviction

Biblical definition of unbelief: absence of Faith, incredulous, skepticism, especially in matters of religious Faith

Faith doesn't need physical proof or evidence to believe. Our foundation [belief system] must be Faith in this truth; it must hold precedence over all we hold fast to without waiver. We must believe in God and that He keeps His word. He is a covenant-keeping God. If He said it, He shall perform it.

This five-letter word doubt is a thief of promise, destiny, and purpose; it will rob you of all that is good. It will steal your confidence it will strip you of your belief in God, defer your hope, and introduce you to anxiety and constant worry, which then opens the door to fear. This devourer of doubt is an enemy of God's design. It lurks around, awaiting the opportunity to strike, always pursuing to conquer and destroy.

Beloved reader, I urge you to put the brakes on doubt, for the thief is robbing us and taking our goods. Stop questioning the truth of God's word. Shut the door, change the locks and let the key of Faith take the lead. This act has to be intentional. Your mind has to be made up. You can be freed from this entanglement. It's possible.

Mark 9:23 Amplified Jesus said to him [you say to me] if you can? All things are possible for the one who believes and trusts in me.

Often, our thoughts supersede the truth as we embrace deceptions that have no evidence to back them up. "You don't understand my struggles; it is my nature. I was raised this way. It's my version of who I am. I've tried to be free." I can continue with the misinformation appearing real as long as we live in the "if" freedom is far away. We can see it from afar, but can we reach it? Walk through it? Apply it? Believe it? Do not allow yourself to be hoodwinked any longer.

Definition of Hoodwink: to deceive or trick

Selah Moment:

Whose report shall you believe?

Why are we so reluctant to believe in the one who is trustworthy who proved He is faithful who accomplished all that He said?

What did God say?

What has He said concerning you?

Who created you? You or him?

Are you ready to follow as He leads?

Are you willing to apply what you have learned so far?

Believe in the power of your thoughts to shape your reality. If you affirm your true self, you will live the life of 'if he can.' Proverbs 23:7 teaches us that our thoughts are the key to our being. It's not about what we say with our mouths but where our hearts truly lie.

The Creator, who crafted the mind and bestowed upon us the ability to think and create, has made it clear in the complexity of our minds that our thoughts can be a reflection of our inner truth. It's crucial to understand that the one who created you knew this and He placed contingencies in His word for this very moment.

This complexity of thought creates double-mindedness. We say one thing with our mouths and believe something contrary in our hearts. What do you think when your heart and mind are not in agreement?

James 1:7-8 For such a person ought not to think or expect that he will receive anything [at all] from the Lord, 8 being a double-minded man, unstable and restless in all his ways [in everything he thinks, feels, or decides].

Our thoughts shape what our hearts will receive and form the falsehood of who we are, not who God says we are, not who we will be. Our reality is, therefore, carried out in our actions and behaviors. What we think impacts who we are and who we will become. I don't know about you, but I played a role for a long time, living a façade and wearing a mask. An actress in the show of my life was created, conducted, and produced by me, myself, and I. I gave myself an Oscar, but I was that delusional. But God had another plan!

What do you do when your mind and heart are not in agreement? It's a problem! What do you tell yourself when you convince yourself of a truth in your mind, but your heart is saying otherwise? It is a tug of war, a wrestling match with no winners.

A mind left unrenewed with God's word produces the opposite of who God says that you are. To become what God says, you must believe Him and not yourself. The false accusation which is contrary to the truth declared over you is the enemy of your soul. It's the thief of destiny and divine purpose. But remember, the power of God's word can transform your thoughts and renew your mind.

2 Corinthians 10:5. We are destroying sophisticated arguments and every exalted and proud thing that sets itself up against the [true] knowledge of God, and we are taking every thought and purpose captive to the obedience of Christ.

The Bible tells us that imaginations left unchecked and arguments not eradicated by God's truth become a fortified fortress in our minds, a stronghold. The battlefield of the mind can only be conquered and defeated with God's word. It's not your words, belief system, or convictions that will free you; it is His. Wrong thinking births a life of disobedience and disconnection, which robs us of our sweet fellowship with our Heavenly Father.

In advance He placed his word, and spoke forth what would be needed as the solution to the problem. He tells us to pull down our reasoning, our imaginations our high-minded thinking, our sophisticated arguments, speculations and lofty things, demolish and tear down. The solution to the problems we face in our thoughts, where the battlefield resides. How do we accomplish this task? We give our minds to God. We read his word to learn his character and in turn learn what he says about us. And most importantly, we seek his presence through prayer, knowing that it brings us closer to Him and His truth. Romans 12:1-2 [amplified] tells us exactly how to do this.

Romans 12:1-2 Therefore I urge you, [b]brothers and sisters, by the mercies of God, to present your bodies [dedicating all of yourselves, set apart] as a living sacrifice, holy and well-pleasing to God, which is your rational (logical, intelligent) act of worship. ² And do not be conformed to this world [any longer with its superficial values and customs], but be [c]transformed and progressively changed [as you mature spiritually] by the renewing of your mind [focusing on godly values and ethical attitudes], so that you may prove [for yourselves] what the will of God is, that which is good and acceptable and perfect [in His plan and purpose for you].

Unfortunately, we have become our own false teachers, false prophets in the story of our lives, corrupting us with what we allow ourselves to believe. We must desire to pick up our weapons, for thoughts are not seen; the action behind the thought is seen; what we don't demolish becomes. God's word is power; it renders our thoughts powerless when we submit them to His word.

Remember the time stated in Eccl 3:2: a time to be born and a time to die. It is time to lay to rest the false narrative and embrace the truth.

Definition of False Narrative: one in which a complete narrative pattern is perceived in a given situation, but it is not an actual narrative at work in the situation or observation. The evidence appears authentic but not accurate at all.

False narratives are created multiple times throughout our day. We see something and begin to form our own understanding of it. We do not stop to check the facts, or the source. Thus, the results reveal our limitations.

The narrative fallacy addresses our limited ability to examine sequences of facts without weaving an explanation into them or, equivalently, forcing a logical link, an arrow of relationship, upon them. Explanations bind facts together, which makes things easier to remember and make sense.

Definition of Narrative: a spoken or written account of connected events. A narrative is not simply a story (although it may be that). Instead, it is a structure for organizing factual claims.

A narrative is a story you write or tell someone, usually in great detail. It can be a work of poetry or prose, or even song, theater, or dance. Often, a narrative is meant to include the "whole story." A summary will give a few key details, and then the narrative will delve into the details.

Selah Moment:
What are you believing about yourself?
What are the false perceptions?
What are the inaccurate assessments?
What is the insufficient and inaccurate information?
What is the false narrative and who told you that?
Did God say it or did you?
Whose voice is the loudest?
What belief system have you embraced that has formed you and created a false reality?

Remember, unless there is agreement, there can never be unity. Your heart and mind are at war. The struggle within, the tug-of-war, is robbing you of your inner peace. Your imagination, your sophisticated arguments with yourself, caused you to be convinced, to believe that this is who you are called to be; this is who you are.

As your heart desires the best version of yourself, you want what you think you want, but your heart says this is what I need: God's will for my life. You convince yourself that what you want is the best, but in reality, only God's truth, His word, tells the tale. He alone has the plan, and what He desires for you and wants to give you is His best. He is the Father who gives His children good gifts, the best gifts. What's a person to do?

Do you remember the season? Come, let us prepare the body for the funeral at hand. Are you ready for it is time! Join me in the death process of our carnal nature, for I promise you the resurrection that takes place will amaze you. Like a volcano hidden under the surface, questions of the soul begin to erupt.

Selah Moment:
What needs to die?
What happened when your thoughts betrayed you?
Are you living a double life of pretense, wearing a mask, pretending to be happy, but in truth, you are screaming on the inside to be free?
What do you do when your soul cries out for God's perfect will for your life?
Can you match God?
Can you outdo him?
Shall you and I continue to live under his grace alone or live in his grace as well?

2 Corinthians 12:9-10 but He has said to me, "My grace is sufficient for you [My lovingkindness and My mercy are more than enough—always available—regardless of the situation]; for [My] power is being perfected [and is completed and

*shows itself most effectively in [your] weakness."
Therefore, I will all the more gladly boast in my
weaknesses, so that the power of Christ [may
completely enfold me and] may dwell in me. So I am
well pleased with weaknesses, with insults, with
distresses, with persecutions, and with difficulties, for
the sake of Christ; for when I am weak [in human
strength], then I am strong [truly able, truly powerful,
truly drawing from God's strength].*

Grace is Divine Love. It is a love like no other. Because there are no conditions for it, we can move through life in harmony with God's direction. We acknowledge that His presence has upheld us in every circumstance. We no longer lean on those things we once did. For it is His power that is made perfect in our weakness.

Definition of Grace: The unmerited gift of divine favor of God towards man. It is the kindness of God that we don't deserve. We didn't earn it; it is a gift from God.

Living under Grace: We are no longer under the law but have been empowered with a new life to live in obedience to it, following Jesus Christ as the King and ruler of our lives.

Living in His Grace: This is a constant realignment of our minds with His word. We see ourselves as God sees us and believe that as we renew our minds, our emotions are transformed, and our behaviors are changed.

Walking in His Grace: Our hearts are open to God's ultimate forgiveness and goodness, and we believe that with His help, we can now walk in grace by obeying and responding to Him in love.

Definition of happiness: The state of well-being a person experiences when good things happen.

Definition of joy: The true definition of joy goes beyond the limited explanation in a dictionary — "a feeling of great pleasure and happiness."

True joy is a transformative, limitless, life-defining, reservoir waiting to be tapped into. It requires the utmost surrender and, like love, is a choice to be made. Joy is of the soul. It transcends moments; it overflows; it runs deep to the core of your being. Joy endures; it's deliberate. Happiness is an outward expression based on happenings; it comes and goes. It's a reaction to a moment in time based on what you are experiencing at that time. More often than not, we want happiness; he wants to give us joy.

The difference between these two words is that one emphasizes Jesus while the other is dependent on self. Happiness is based on what is happening in our lives. If good things are happening, then we are happy. A job promotion – we are so glad! Marriage – we are delighted! A new house – oh boy, are we happy!

And now, we lose our job – not happy! Our marriage ends – happy is nowhere to be found. The new house becomes a financial burden, and selling it is the only way to alleviate that stress. I can guarantee happiness has left the building! Happiness requires our emotions to align with what feels good. Happiness can be one moment and suddenly not. It does not remain. It is not unmovable. Happiness can be shaken.

Joy remains in the good times and bad times. It's a constant state of being. It's not based on feelings but on reliance on the Father.

Joy abides in hope. It dwells richly in our hearts. It's ever-present. Amid pain, death of a loved one, sickness in your baby, isolation, rejection, abandonment, poverty, and lack it remains, it enables you to hold on to gain strength when you want to give up. Why? Because your heart is convinced of God's unchanging hands, you have an unmovable assurance in his word. You do not waiver based on your circumstances.

Joy is abiding. It's remaining in the hope. It's secured not in what is tangible but in what is intangible. It's not moved by mere feelings or words or self-gratification. Its assurance is foundationally entwined in our savior's hope and presence.

Joy is in total dependence on Jesus. Like the song mentioned previously, "None But Jesus," happiness depends on moments created and expressed outwardly; happiness is external expression.

Joy is within and cannot be robbed, taken, or displaced. Joy is knowing your savior and rejoicing in him.

...The joy of the Lord is your strength and stronghold. Nehemiah 8:10.

Despite your thoughts, tragedy, chaos, and storms of life, one thing remains. In the pain when you can't breathe, one thing remains a constant in your heart: God's faithfulness. You are convinced of the truth of his word that all things work together for your good. Why? Because you love Him and because He loves you. Your pain and suffering are tools in your Heavenly Father's hands to shape and mold you to become more like him. It's a character builder to reflect and create the image of Christ in you.

So, what needs to die? **Expectation in others!**

The expectation is for others to meet the needs of true fulfillment that only Christ can give. As we embrace and bring to death things hindering our inner growth, only then can the birthing of who He desires us to be come forth.

John 16:22 tells us no one can take our joy from us. What an assurance to hold on to no matter what comes our way. The truth is embraced, believed, and celebrated—our focus shifts. His word constantly renews our minds. We make it a practice in our daily lives. We become convinced, confident that through it all, He shall, has, and will remain.

If I summarize here, the song that comes to mind is Through It All by Andrae Crouch. I once believed that problems came to annoy and cause me grief and pain. But I've learned to trust that the plan of the Most High God is all-inclusive. Every emotion, every pain, every joy, He knows it. And no matter what I may try to do to solve a situation, His way is always best. He is dependable, trustworthy, and ever-present. No other shall do; His word never fails. He promises never to leave us, and He doesn't! Nothing else in this world holds that assurance.

In this life, nothing is permanent. But oh, the love of Jesus, what can compare? When misunderstood, He understands. When others don't see you, He does. He is the friend that sticks closer than any brother, sister, mother, Father, son, or daughter. You become persuaded by only one thing.

*In Romans 8:31-39, **31,** What then shall we say to these things? If God is for us, who can be against us? **32** He who did not spare His own Son, but delivered Him up for us all, how shall He not with Him also freely give us all things? **33** Who shall bring* *a charge against God's elect? It is God who justifies. 34 Who is he who condemns? It is Christ who died, and furthermore is also risen, who is even at the right hand of God, who also makes intercession for us. 35 Who shall separate us from the love of Christ? Shall tribulation, or distress, or persecution, or famine, or nakedness, or peril, or sword? 36 As it is written: "For Your sake we are killed all day long; We are accounted as sheep for the slaughter." 37 Yet in all these things, we are more than conquerors through Him who loved us. 38 For I am persuaded that neither death nor life, nor angels nor principalities nor powers, nor things present nor things to come, 39 nor height nor depth, nor any other created thing, shall be able to separate us from the love of God which is in Christ Jesus our Lord.*

His Word of Promise becomes legitimate. The accuser is made silent. Nothing and no one can condemn you, trouble cannot rattle you, calamity cannot break you, sickness cannot deter you, or the death of a loved one shake you. You remain like flint, anchored in His unending unshakeable love.

Despite all you endure, the victory is in Jesus Christ, your savior, friend, and King, the true lover of your soul. What or who can measure or compare to this great love? This truth liberates; it brings freedom, no longer captive to others' opinions of you. No more people-pleasing performances are to be accepted. You are loved now and always.

What needs to die? **People-pleasing mindset!**

God is for us, He is with us, and we are not alone. We will never be forsaken. He has justified and called us to himself. He is all that we need. People in our lives are an extension of his love, a gift to enjoy, but our God is the source, the substance, and the constant that remains.

When I think of the goodness of God, I sometimes get a picture that helps me as a visual learner. Now hear me; God is so much bigger than my feeble mind can comprehend, but in my limitation and simplicity of soul, he speaks to me in simplistic ways so I may understand. In my time of reflection, He brought to my remembrance a Sunday school lesson I did that involved an ice cream sundae. There's a revelation to be realized.

Definition of Sundae: A dish of ice cream served with various toppings.

When you prepare a sundae, there is no limit to what you can add. But before adding to it, you must begin with the show's star. The very center of it all. The ice cream! Jesus is at the center of it all!

Once the ice cream is securely placed, it is easy to add to it, such as fruit, candy, sauces, nuts, cookies, marshmallows, or whipped cream, to name a few. All of this goodness is added once the center is placed. Sound familiar – Matthew 6:33 paraphrased says Seek first [ice cream first] …..and all these things will be added to you. We are a sundae in the making. Each one is uniquely designed.

What makes the sundae so delicious is hidden underneath all those fixings: the ice cream! Without the ice cream in between all that gooey deliciousness, you just have fruit with sauce. No, no, no. I want the ice cream. Ice cream is the center of it all. It makes the sundae worth eating.

Now, I am trying to convey this: The fruit, the cherry, the sauce, and the trimmings are all extensions of God's love in our lives. It's the extras, the people, the stuff, but the ice cream is his love. The ice cream complements the flavors of the trimmings. It brings it to another level. Do you understand my metaphor? Without the ice cream, is it a sundae? Without God's love, can you experience the enjoyment he desires for you?

We tend to be satisfied with just the trimmings, living out our lives in the comfortability of the sundae we created based on our knowledge of what a sundae is in our mind's eye. Some of us never get to experience an actual sundae in the way that the creator and inventor created it to be experienced. But when the epiphany occurs, the experience is heightened and taken to another level that blows our minds. Now I know what some of you are saying! It's not all that it's just a sundae. But I did say this was a Sunday School lesson.

As for me, who is lactose intolerant, it's not a big deal. But imagine, for a moment, a child who has never had a "sundae" experience; their surprise and awe as they place all the ingredients in their mouth for the first time. Their little eyes seem to pop out of their sockets as the explosion of flavors takes place like firecrackers in their mouth. They will never look at ice cream the same way again.

I say all that to say this: childlike faith is needed to embrace all that your Heavenly Father desires to shower upon you. See Him as the adoring Father that He is. One of love who so desires to lavish you with the best gifts, but often, we hold on to our best, not realizing it is not His best for us. The very word needed for our transformation. It's time for the restoration of our soul.

Romans 10:17 says: So faith comes from hearing [what is told], and what is heard comes by the [preaching of the] message concerning Christ.

Selah Moment:

Can you perceive this moment at hand, the message to be heard and received that comes through the message of Jesus Christ?

Are you prepared to let go of what you have been holding on to so tightly?

Are you willing to release it all to him?

To empty yourself of all your preconceived ideas of self and allow him to fashion you into the vessel of great honor for His use?

Are you satisfied with just existing or do you want to experience the abundant life?

Are you ready to put to death all that is holding you back from experiencing the wonderful life awaiting you in him?

Are you content with just the trimmings or are you ready to begin with the ice cream, the very center of this masterpiece and then allow the Lord to add all that is necessary?

Personal Reflections:

A time to plant and a time to uproot what is planted. A time to kill and a time to heal; A time to tear down and a time to build up. Ecc 3:2-3

I spoke earlier about the foundation, which is your faith in Jesus Christ. Now, we can tackle a time to break down uproot and a time to build up, a time to plant, and a time to pluck up what is planted. Walk with me as we dig deeper into the way to find the truth!

Matthew 7:24-25 The Two Foundations
"So everyone who hears these words of Mine and acts on them, will be like a wise man [a far-sighted, practical, and sensible man] who built his house on the rock. And the rain fell, and the floods and torrents came, and the winds blew and slammed against that house; yet it did not fall, because it had been founded on the rock. And everyone who hears these words of Mine and does not do them, will be like a foolish (stupid) man who built his house on the sand. ²⁷ And the rain fell, and the floods and torrents came, and the winds blew and slammed against that house; and it fell—and great and complete was its fall."

The Wise Builder	**The Foolish Builder**
Faith in Christ	Faith in Self – Self Sufficient
Applies the word	Does not apply
Believes and lives it out	Does not live it out

The wise builder considered wisdom. Wisdom is available to us in every aspect of life. Faith is filtered through the lenses of God's word, believed and lived out by Faith. We must build on the foundation of Faith in His word and not our own words. I built on the foundation of fear and not Faith for a long time.

F alse
E vidence
A ppearing
R eal

There was a time when I was unwilling to tear down what I had built because of the time and labor I put into making myself, building my persona, and my self-reliance. I put a lot of time in, buddy!

Designing the house's structure took great detail, and choosing the right exterior to make it look pretty took place without ever assessing the foundation. Well, by now, you can guess what happened. I believed in what I could see. Faith was nowhere to be found. When the storm of life came, it all came tumbling down. What happened to my Academy Award performance? Do you remember it in Chapter 2? It became a shambles under my feet.

The life I built could not withstand the pressure of disappointments. Only then did I realize that I never took stock or assessed and never took the time to consider whether my foundation was solid? I was confident in my reliance on self-image, building myself with my understanding; nothing else was considered. I focused on all the wrong things and never once thought about the foundation, never mind if I was even on one.

And when it all came crashing down, who did I blame? The very one I did not consider or believe in! We didn't even have a conversation or make the introduction, and yet I lashed out, and He is to blame. I could not save myself. What a big surprise! I couldn't see it, blinded by my ways, and thought I missed this key component necessary for the house to stand. Jesus Christ, my rock!

He is the foundation. And a house cannot stand without a foundation. It's not sturdy; it will not hold up to the weight or structure. Faith was the key, but it was nowhere to be found.

God had to tear down to build up. He had to uproot and pluck out before He could plant. The land of my heart had to be excavated and removed from the weeds of unmet expectations, as I willingly transferred ownership to the rightful owner. My self-reliance was demolished as my trust and reliance I now placed upon my savior.

It was time to bring in the structural engineer, Jesus Christ, who is qualified to inspect the foundation of our lives. He alone sees the cracks and potential issues before calamity strikes. The circumstances that were to bring hopelessness and despair brought forth a great triumph. The persona that took so much of my time to build, now stripped away, no longer held the same value in my eyes as it once did. I had to begin again. But this time, Jesus Christ revealed that the foundation had been laid all along.

All he desired to build now was a structure that could withstand any future storm. What I once believed to be a curse was a blessing in disguise. See, the devil plotted, schemed, and conspired to destroy and crush, but God had a plan. The foundation has already been laid. Thank God for deliverance!

How grateful I am now for the storm; I can now embrace, accept, and appreciate the instrument of life's woes, becoming a triumph in the scene we call life. As Faith unfolded before my very eyes, to my surprise all along, now revealed. A measure of Faith is given to everyone as He reminded me of His truth.

Romans 12:3 For by the grace [of God] given to me I say to everyone of you not to think more highly of himself [and of his importance and ability] than he ought to think; but to think so as to have sound judgment, as God has apportioned to each a degree of Faith [and a purpose designed for service].

Faith was now securely in place; the very foundation needed all along before building. Faith in my Heavenly Father to uphold, keep, and deliver. He said we can build, and now my labor will not be in vain—much to ponder and consider. I implore you to consider the cost before building, for unless the Lord builds the house, we will labor in vain. Build yourself up in the Faith, upon the rock of Jesus Christ, and you will stand.

Selah Moment:

What is our current foundation built on?

Do we know?

Does our foundation have cracks that need to be fixed? What are the weeds of life choking the seed of Faith that wants to grow?

Can we discern?

Can we assess what foundation the house is built upon? What's holding us up?

For the seed of God's word to be planted, what must God tear down, break apart, uproot, and pluck out ?

When the storms of life shake us to the core, beloved, shall we stand?

What storm has taken you off course?

Do we blame God when our mindset, perception, and false reality are shattered?

Are we trusting in His word or ourselves?

Are we confronted with Faith or fear?

Is God's word the solid foundation we are resting on?

In God's mercy, I am so grateful for the stages of rain that He allowed. The same rain that can soothe and bring forth crops in my life is the same rain that can destroy. The intensity of that rain determines the impact. The rains of my daily troubles and concerns are manageable through the conviction of God's word.

The unexpected storms, tsunamis, floods of catastrophic events, such as divorce, cancer, death of loved ones, homelessness, betrayal, abandonment, and verbal abuse had to be uprooted and plucked out. I am indebted for the storms filtered through God's hands that saw what I could not see and uprooted what was killing me.

What appeared as a curse, a detriment, a loss was a gain. It had a purpose! God sent the storm to rebuild, shape, and solidify the structure. It made the foundation on which my life was now being built strong, firm, and unmovable.

You see, life will have many troubles, storms will come, and rains will fall, but when God is your shield, you feel only what He allows. The impact is not to destroy; it's to build and make you anew.

Did I mention that the goal of our journey is to make us like His son? In the life lived in Christ, there will constantly be tearing down, building up, death, rebirth, joy, sorrow, mourning, and dancing, but how we view our Heavenly Father and how we choose to believe will determine how we react when it comes.

Trials come. What shall we choose? Will we allow God to shape us and make us better, or will we surrender to our thoughts and allow life's troubles to birth in us a bitter root? Better or Bitter. The only difference is the "I" that must die! See, we always have a choice.

Believing in his word should be the position of our hearts for us to be empowered. Our focus is not on the storm or the impact it leaves behind, not that we don't hurt, not that we are not afraid, not that at times we feel lost, can't see, can't breathe, in a fog, no, no, we are human.

Sometimes, life throws you an unwanted curve ball. When it hits, you feel the sting. It's okay to cry to say ouch. You have the bruise as evidence of the impact, but wait, he is the solution. Are there any curve balls in your life that could use an ice pack to help take away the sting? God is the ultimate healer.

Psalms 147:3 says, He heals the brokenhearted And binds up their wounds [healing their pain and comforting their sorrow].

The promise of His word that we must choose to believe by Faith is that we will not be destroyed; we will not be shaken from our original position because we are on the foundation of His word. He is our rock.

Our lives must be founded on Faith in Him, a life worth living.

Instead of complaining, count it all joy. You're being remodeled, and who doesn't like a remodel? Who wouldn't want change? New furniture, new painted walls and finishes, new bathroom, new roof, brand new furnace, granite, or quartz countertops?

Surrender to Him; take Him at his word. Believe in what He has spoken, and you will be able to say I am more than a conqueror. So next time a storm comes your way, remember He's making adjustments and repairs to secure and strengthen your Faith.

Let Him seal up the cracks in the foundation that you wouldn't know were there if the flood didn't come. You know the last season's cracks of unforgiveness, anger, fear, and bitterness. That season when you were getting divorced, lost your mother, and became homeless with two kids. Yes, when life happened, the tsunami came, and it revealed something in your life you never thought existed.

The rain exposes the grudges and all the records of wrongs embedded in your heart, all once hidden. The storm and the revelation it brings are not to harm you. It's to build you up, to make you brand new. Who else but your Creator knows? He sees. He understands. He created you. Your original design cannot be fabricated or added upon. He knows exactly who He created you to be in Him.

It's time to uproot so He can build in you the solid foundation that will withstand the upcoming rains, storms, and tsunamis of life. After you have yielded to his unchanging hand and allowed his grace to seal the cracks, you shall remain steadfast when the floods come. You will survive, you will become stronger.

Remember, surgery hurts; it never feels good. Recovery is painful, but God's word is the anesthesia and the pain reliever, cutting and healing simultaneously. It's the treatment given in those agonizing moments in time that prevents us from feeling the actual impact. The pain we feel when our emotions are intensified is manageable when He is in it. I feel you. I know it hurts; take a deep breath. It's been so long; breathe, and you are not alone.

John 16:33 says: I have told you these things, so that in Me you may have [perfect] peace. In the world you have tribulation and distress and suffering, but be courageous [be confident, be undaunted, be filled with joy]; I have overcome the world." [My conquest is accomplished, My victory abiding.]

He never promised we would not have troubles in this life. He promised that we would not walk in them or through them alone. Let His word bring forth the confidence needed. He is letting you know He has overcome the world; He has overcome all that is in it. Therefore, the Christ in you shall give you the strength to become an overcomer.

Definition of Overcomer: a person who overcomes something and succeeds in dealing with or gaining control of some problem or difficulty.

Prayer:

I pray Lord, help me to convey the truth you placed in me in a way that is understood. Help your readers see you. Help them to desire, to want to know you.

Let this not be just mere words that brings comfort but let your words come off the pages and transform lives. Let your word have the long-lasting effect needed to cause the blind to see, as the captive is free.

No longer slaves of mindsets created by self or others. No longer desiring to live in the dysfunction and lies that have been embraced and kept us bound.

Father you are Almighty. You have already spoken forth your word. You said when you created us male and female it was good. Holy Spirit unveil the eyes to grasp this truth. Make it alive!

Let it go forth and penetrate into the mind, thought and imagination. Let it pull down all that once hindered for your truth to become. Let the activation of your word bring forth your desired end in which you have purposed before the foundation of the earth.

All power and authority are in your hands. There is nothing you cannot do. You are the miraculous God. You can do all things.

By faith I ask you now to shatter the thoughts, cast down, pull off, and remove all that once hindered. Let every lie, mindset and imagination that once was exalted above your word be destroyed.

Let your word become alive in your child who is reading the words on this page. Reveal yourself and make them anew. Form in them your desire and purpose and original intent. In Jesus' name, son of the Living God, Amen

Personal Reflections:

_____
_____
_____
_____
_____
_____
_____
_____
_____
_____
_____
_____
_____
_____
_____
_____
_____
_____
_____
_____
_____
_____
_____
_____
_____

A time to weep and a time to laugh; A time to mourn and a time to dance. Ecc 3:4

Dialogue with God:

My child this is the time for me to kill the fear. This is the time for me to heal your brokenness. No more weeping for this is the time to laugh. No more mourning for it is time to dance. It's time to put to death the thought process in your life that's robbing you of your joy and faith in me. It's time to allow my word to remove once and for all what has been killing your soul.

Definition of Soul: the spiritual or immaterial part of a human being or animal, regarded as immortal. Pneuma [πνεῦμα] is an ancient Greek word for "breath", and in a religious context for "spirit" or "soul". People don't have a soul—they are a soul. They are a "nephesh," a living, breathing, physical being. To love the Lord with your soul is to offer your entire being, with no limitations.

Genesis 2:7 Then the Lord God [a]formed [that is, created the body of] man from the [b]dust of the ground, and breathed into his nostrils the breath of life; and the man became a living being [an individual complete in body and spirit]. 2:7)

The soul is not some irrelevant spiritual body; it is you and I, all of us, our whole being or self. The chains that bound the soul are meant to be broken. Jesus Christ came to set the captives free. Did someone share with you this good news that He is the anointed one that destroys, not just breaks every yoke; not some yokes, but every yoke? Today, you have been told of the great news of your freedom. Finally, debt-free. No more bankruptcy, no outstanding creditors, no longer broke but rich beyond compare. Jesus, our Savior and King, paid it on our behalf. What we perceive as giants in our lives are pebbles in God's hands. It's time to align our emotions with God's word. It's time to recognize and kill the giants in our lives.

A brother in Christ, David Carruthers, wrote a book, Kill Your Giants. This book had so many tidbits that aided me throughout the years. I read the book long ago, but in the mourning season, God brought the treasures obtained through his wisdom to the surface. What was hidden in my heart came forth in my hour of need. I have great news to share with you at this moment. The seed of faith in God's word is active and alive; it's always working in our lives.

Prayer became my lifestyle during my season of effective prayer in seeking God. It was the season when those around me became annoyed with all my praying. Every opportunity granted, all I wanted to do was pray. I thank God for the people He sometimes sent to aid, strengthen, and guide me on my quest. The excellent deposit was placed, birthing intercession and prayer. He sent Jen, a sister from my church, long ago. I'm grateful for the instrument she was in the hands of my Father.

I've understood that when God has a specific purpose, He will give you what you need to accomplish that purpose. God desires to make us successful. His aspiration for us is to thrive and push us forward to new heights in Him as we excel in greatness.

Devotion to seeking Him has yielded my greatest reward, for that season was what kept me in this season of drought. When I couldn't pray or read the word to find strength, the reserve of what I had done in previous seasons kept me in my now.

On January 18, 2021, my life changed in a way that, if not for God, I would not have recovered. My dearest husband said his last words, Jesus! Jesus! Jesus, and took his final breath in my arms. For without warning, a massive heart attack silenced him forevermore. What started as asthma became more than anticipated. I am still struggling with the memory.

In my mourning stage, my God was 'the enough' needed to strengthen me when strength was lost. Friends couldn't do anything, family couldn't aid, and no one understood but Jesus. I could not be reached. I was lost to the despondency of my own thoughts and emotions. Jesus reached into my darkness and pulled me out.

The God who sees saw what would be, and He set things up and placed people strategically to be a source of comfort and to aid me in my darkest moments. When I couldn't pray, my spirit interceded. When I couldn't get out of bed, my soul sang lyrics and songs that reminded me of God's goodness.

In the time of my most incredible pain and suffering, more painful than previous trials, His Word of Promise carried me through. The prayers prayed all those years ago, the deposits placed in the bank of God's kingdom I could now withdraw. My soul was comforted in the darkest night when it was hard to breathe.

Now hear me: I'm not saying I didn't have a support system because I did. God sent wonderful people my way to aid and strengthen in the natural. When I didn't want to cook, my daughter and my best friend, my sister in Christ, looked after me. When I didn't want to get out of bed, I was encouraged to get up and lift my countenance to remember the truth. Not my truth at the moment of my loss, not my truth in the pain that was trying to take my breath, no God's truth.

I had sisters in Christ who sacrificed time on my behalf in my hour of need. Many gave me what I wanted, but on one particular day, my greatest need was prayer. And God ordered the steps of His child, Diane.

I mention her because many were impactful and raised to aid, comfort, and support, and yes, I am eternally grateful for the part God had them play. I must bring emphasis to this act. I am compelled to because it was what was most important for the subject at hand.

There's a story in the Bible about Mary and Martha. They loved the Lord, but their worship was shown in different ways. Both esteemed Him and displayed gratitude and love for Him.

Luke 10:40-42 says But Martha was very busy and distracted with all of her serving responsibilities; and she approached Him and said, "Lord, is it of no concern to You that my sister has left me to do the serving alone? Tell her to help me and do her part." 41 But the Lord replied to her, "Martha, Martha, you are worried and bothered and anxious about so many things; 42 but only one thing is necessary, for Mary has chosen the good part [that which is to her advantage], which will not be taken away from her."

What was it that Mary chose to do that will remain? She chose to sit at the savior's feet. That was her worship to Him. Mary discovered the importance of what her soul truly needed. The good part is what's preserved in the Bank of Heaven.

Matthew 6:20 says But store up for yourselves treasures in heaven, where neither moth nor rust destroys, and where thieves do not break in and steal;

Does that mean our Lord didn't appreciate Martha and her sacrifice? Not at all. But Mary recognized her need, Jesus. Not to please Him by doing but by communing instead.

My soul was parched. Though food and company were appreciated, my soul needed prayer. My soul was having great difficulty. I wanted to give up; I was tired of the fight. The enemy was quietly chiseling away my confidence and hope. Slowly but surely, in the quietness of my soul, I was losing hope again. I was drowning, and Diane threw me a lifeline—so appreciative! It brought to my remembrance my first love.

In previous pages, I spoke of what we needed to kill, like our giants. I will now name one of my giants at that moment: **depression**.

After the loss of my mom on October 26, 2016, undetected sorrow securely latched itself secretly. My faith was diminishing unbeknown to me. The unwillingness to grieve and mourn properly had an aftermath effect in 2021. The compiling sorrows became too much for my bruised heart to bear. I could not hold up under the weight. The very existence of "why am I here" haunted my thoughts.

After so many disappointments, I was tired and weary and willingly wanted to give up the fight. I stopped looking towards the horizon, the rainbow after the storm, the life of cards dealt brought forth fury. I didn't understand, and in that moment of despair and confusion, the fog I was under started to clear. In my season of mourning, I became unveiled to many truths, my giants, **perceptions, mistakes, and displaced hope**.

In the book of Numbers 13, we have a giant scenario. Twelve spies were sent forth into the land of Canaan to spy out the land to inhabit. God himself confirmed His desires to Moses. He told Moses his will. He specifically said to send twelve to spy and scout the land he was giving to them. He said to pick one from each tribe. Moses sought guidance from the Lord before acting. He understood his need for God's Divine leading. Do we?

Is God the first person we seek after when making important, critical decisions, or do we succumb to our own ways and wisdom? This is food for thought. Okay, back to the story.

The 12 Spies were chosen, one from each tribe, to go and gather information. Moses gave specific instructions. Those inhabiting the land are they many? Were they strong or weak? Was the city open camps or fortifications? Was the land productive or poor, fruitful or barren? Moses also instructed them to bring back evidence of the fruit of the land, strong or weak, few or many. Only two of the twelve scouts sent forth had a different report. Ten perceived and were convinced of what they saw, which altered their belief system. Their observation of self was likened to grasshoppers and the squatters as giants.

Definition of Squatter: a person who unlawfully occupies unused land, one who has no legal claim, no title, no lease, no rights

Why did I use the word squatter? Because God is the owner. He is the creator. Everything, and I mean everything, belongs to him. And if you are not given the deed to inhabit the land, then you are an official squatter!

Psalms 24:1 The earth [b]is the Lord's, and the fullness of it. The world and those who dwell in it.

Our battles belong to the Lord. The act of obedience to God's word brings forth the victory. We are already triumphant; we have to walk it out. We put too much weight on the information of others, the assessment obtained, or what is shown and perceived. We tend to make decisions based not on fact or God's word but on our ideas, thoughts, and wisdom. We make the truth we hear suffocate the truth of what God said.

Our perception is the obstacle. We embrace the false reality. Our truth says that they are giants. We assess based on a low opinion of self because we don't know who we are. We displaced our God-given identity and lost our original passport. We have amnesia. A spiritual brain injury has occurred!

Definition of passport: "any travel document issued by competent authority showing **the bearer's origin, identity**, and nationality, if any, which is valid for the entry of the bearer into a foreign country.

Definition of Amnesia: a partial or total loss of memory.

We've forgotten who we are, who God said we are, and who we belong to. Ephesians 2:10, paraphrased, says we have an intimate relationship with the King of Kings and Lord of Lords. We are His workmanship—His masterwork, a work of art created in Christ Jesus.

Citizens of Heaven, we are not lost. We still need to remember. His truth says we are His children created in His image. Before He formed you and me, He knew us. Before we came to be, He set us apart. We are chosen, God's special possession.

Perception is another giant we need to kill. We see, hear, and gain awareness through our senses. We rely on that to guide us, convinced by what we see. The giant before us, based on what we have discerned as a giant, supersedes the Almighty, all-powerful God, the creator of the giants seen, the one who is more than able to defeat all foes of our soul. What we believe is what we will act upon.

Aren't these the same children that God delivered from Egypt? After 400 years in slavery, an impossible task made possible by the God we serve. These are the same people He caused the angel of death to pass by while their enemies suffered significant consequences. The same children stood witness to the parting of the sea; the same children fed supernaturally in the wilderness—all the evidence needed on how great, vast, limitless, capable, and efficient this God was. The God who is all-knowing didn't know about the squatters occupying the land?

The same God delivered me from past pain, divorce, difficult circumstances, and homelessness, and yet the giant before me displaced my hope. Was I, in my wilderness and mourning, able to acknowledge that my destiny and purpose were not derailed based on my current state and feelings? For a moment, I forgot who I was and what God said!

What did he say? It was his will; he had already given the land to them. He said the land was theirs not will be or might be. They had the deed but did not believe it. They trusted in what they saw and not what God said or did. Can we acknowledge? Their inheritance is stated in God's word. The land was given before they came upon it.

Definition of Inheritance: to receive an irrevocable gift, "emphasizing the special relationship between the benefactor and the recipients. A spiritual promise from God is an irrevocable gift.

We are co-heirs to the promise, having been justified by His grace as we receive all He has promised by faith. We are part of God's Heavenly Kingdom, a promise that the enemy will never be able to steal. His word will never be reversed or refuted concerning those who believe. No more excellent gift can ever be bestowed than to be engrafted into the family of God. The one who promised alone can revoke or bring forth a forfeit, and He said it was His will. He said this belonged to you.

In Journey Of The Bride, Seek Ye First Volume I, I expounded on the story of Abraham and Sarah. When the test of obedience came, the very thing promised and given now had to be sacrificed, but it was accredited to Abraham's faith; he believed in God's word. He believed in what was promised. The same God that gave him what was impossible in his eyes is the same God that could resurrect what appears to be dead. The desire longed for, waited so long for, and God wanted to take it away. Faith and obedience go hand in hand. The test of life is a tool in the savior's hands to build in you and me the character needed to weather all future storms: Faith!

Hopelessness, depression, anger; the giant squatters occupying my thoughts and heart needed to be killed!

Selah Moment:

What happened to what God said?

Did he not say it was his will and that the land was theirs?

That he had given it to them?

Was he confused on who was occupying the land?

Was he surprised that the land had squatters on it?

Are you able to identify the squatters, the giants?

What have you allowed the enemy of your thoughts and emotions to take from you illegally?

What have you allowed the devil to steal from you that is rightfully yours?

What did God say?

Who is on the property of your heart?

Who has the deed?

Who is the rightful owner?

Do you have the unwavering faith to trust in the promise given and the God who made it?

What is God asking you to sacrifice right now?

What is he putting his finger on?

What triggers are causing a reaction at this very moment?

What are your forgotten promises from God?

What squatters have you allowed to stay or remain on the land of your heart and mind?

During this season, in this ultimate test, I've come to understand that to obtain the promise of God's will [Isaac], my will [Ishmael] had to be removed. To be clear, this was the testing of my Faith.

Remember James 1:2-4 says: Consider it nothing but joy, my brothers and sisters, whenever you fall into various trials. Be assured that the testing of your faith [through experience] produces endurance [leading to spiritual maturity, and inner peace] And let endurance have its perfect result and do a thorough work, so that you may be perfect and completely developed [in your faith], lacking in nothing.

Trust me, I did not consider it joy at that moment, but over time, it has become the strength needed to continue waiting upon the Lord and His promises to me. And I am still awaiting the promise of my God even as I write. What promise are you still waiting for God to fulfill?

The abundant life God promised is in His will. We can't cry for His will [Isaac] while still holding on to our will [Ishmael]. Let go, say goodbye. There is a requirement, and there is no way around it, God's will or ours! What shall it be? Are you ready to say yes? It's time to cross over. No more bartering with God asking if you can bring some things you collected in Egypt. You and I cannot bear fruit if we are not abiding in him, for he is the vine; we are the branches. It's by His Spirit.

Do you want sweet, juicy fruit, or are you satisfied with the thorns and thistles produced by your thoughts, emotions, and will? The squatters you have allowed to take ownership, inhabit, and occupy are idols. You cannot inherit the land of your heart until you are willing to cast down the idols erected. No more residents; your heart is his home. What once was left unoccupied is your soul. Can your squatters be the pain you carry from divorce, adultery, fornication, pornography, the painful experience of having an abortion, the pain of sexual abuse, gossip, alcohol, addictive behaviors, anger, past failures, eating disorders, negative words people have said or friends struggling with drugs? Are you able to identify those things in you that are occupying your soul? Stop weeping for what was lost.

If we are honest with ourselves, our will causes more harm than good. Yes, we had moments, stages and seasons of happiness but did it really satisfy? My season of weeping is coming to an end. I have no more tears left. I have worn myself out. My emotions have placed a heavy toll, a heavy burden that I now desire to discard willingly, no fight here. I'm spent, I desire to dance. I want to laugh. I want joy. So, if that means, Lord not my will but your will be done then bring it on. I'm happy to sing so long and farewell.

Remember that journal mentioned earlier, feel free to add your own squatters!

The spiritual squatters of our hearts now get the eviction notice needed. How do we identify squatters? See a few to ponder below.

Sample Squatters:
Your identity perceived by self
Your accomplishments
Your lustful desire
Your job
Your friends of bad influence
Your material possessions
Your chosen mate, not the one God chose for you
Your wisdom
Your fear of failure
Your intelligence
Your Pride
Your self-condemnation
Your closed-mindedness
Your eating disorders
Your poor self-image, unworthiness
Your educational accomplishments held in higher esteem than Godly wisdom
Your will and all that is contrary to the will of God

Selah Moment:

Are you ready to let the self-condemnation, pride of self-reliance, and unworthiness go?

Your spiritual inheritance is connected to the kingdom of God, and you are a child of God's kingdom. So, who has the deed to your heart?

Doesn't the deed state the actual ownership?

Do you believe who the rightful owner is?

Are you convinced of your inheritance, or do you doubt it?

If you ask your Heavenly Father, will he not remind you?

Do you want to know?

Do you willingly forfeit by punishing yourself for past mistakes, holding onto your lack of self-worth?

Do you not know? Hasn't anyone told you that the blood of Christ applied over your life has redeemed you?

If God made a promise, can anyone revoke that promise?

If the room of your soul is filled, is there room for the Holy Spirit? The room does not belong to them.

Can you see that they are illegally dwelling?

What is he saying to you right now?

Is he bringing to your remembrance things forgotten?

Is He making sense of some things right now?

Definition of Illegal: contrary to or in violation of a law

Definition of deed: legal document that is signed giving ownership of property or legal rights deed promise given from God

Definition of Forfeit: loss through transgression or non-observance of some law or rule. To lose or lose the right to especially by some error, offense or crime.

Matthew 11:28 Come to Me, all who are weary and heavily burdened [by religious rituals that provide no peace], and I will give you rest [refreshing your souls with salvation].

Confess now and release all your burdens. Trust Him, for he promised us in His word. Stop beating yourself up. Stop believing the lie; you did not forfeit unless He told said that you did.

1John 1:9 If we [freely] admit that we have sinned and confess our sins, He is faithful and just [true to His own nature and promises], and will forgive our sins and cleanse us continually from all unrighteousness [our wrongdoing, everything not in conformity with His will and purpose].

Do you know where the deed is? Have you lost it or misplaced it? Guess what, even if you did. Your position does not negate what God has said. All it brings is delay on your part, not His. If God said it, it shall surely come to pass. Even when you don't feel qualified, even when you don't feel you deserve it, God still promised. Nothing you can do, no mistake, lack of faith, doubt, or regret can change that. God still gave it. See, He gave it to you before you beheld it, before you asked for it, before you acknowledged you even needed it.

The deed is the promise of God, a testament to His infinite power and wisdom. He, who is all-knowing and all-powerful, had you and me in mind when He made this promise. He gave it to you in advance, even before you said yes, because He knew what you would need in your future. He understood what would be necessary for you to achieve your fullest potential.

God's plan for you was not a spontaneous decision, but a carefully premeditated one. Before your eyes, mind, and heart were even open to the idea of saying yes, He had already given you His best, the gift of His love.

Some of us have asked our Heavenly Father for true love, and some of us are still waiting for it to come to pass. If you are having a hard time receiving His love, how can you identify true love, let alone receive it and accept it?

We sometimes assess in our own understanding what we think we need to make us happy. We come up short and are left wanting. The longing of our hearts is never quenched.

Happiness does not sustain; it is not what we need. We look everywhere for it without success. Joy is what helps us stay the course, as mentioned earlier. The joy of the Lord is our strength! It is a gift from God and available to us as we seek Him.

Shall we finally throw off the entanglement of happiness and instead embrace the fullness of joy that comes in His Presence?

Selah Moment:

Can you recognize His presence?

Can you identify the workings of His hands in your life?

Have you ever considered that your prayers could produce evidence right before your eyes?

Embrace the promise of new beginnings. Surrender your continual state of mourning; the deep sorrow choking the life source within. More giants to kill! Stop covering yourself with the **regrets**, stop wearing the garments of **disappointment and lost hope**. Take it off for God has prepared for you new garments.

Colossians 3:10-17 and have put on the new [spiritual] self who is being continually renewed in true knowledge in the image of Him who created the new self— a renewal in which there is no [distinction between] Greek and Jew, circumcised and uncircumcised, [nor between nations whether] [a]barbarian or [b]Scythian, [nor in status whether] slave or free, but Christ is all, and in all [so believers are equal in Christ, without distinction]. So, as God's own chosen people, who are holy [set apart, sanctified for His purpose] and well-beloved [by God Himself], put on a heart of compassion, kindness, humility, gentleness, and patience [which has the power to endure whatever injustice or unpleasantness comes, with good temper]; bearing graciously with one another, and willingly forgiving each other if one has a cause for complaint against another; just as the Lord has forgiven you, so should you forgive. Beyond all these things put on and wrap yourselves in [unselfish] love, which is the perfect bond of unity [for everything is bound together in agreement when each one seeks the best for others]. Let the peace of Christ [the inner calm of one who walks daily with Him] be the controlling factor in your hearts [deciding and settling questions that arise]. To this peace indeed you were called as members in one body [of believers]. And be thankful [to God always]. Let the [spoken] word of Christ have its home within you [dwelling in your heart and mind—permeating every aspect of your being] as you teach [spiritual things] and admonish and train one another with all wisdom, singing psalms and hymns and spiritual songs with thankfulness in your hearts to God. Whatever you do [no matter what it is] in word or deed, do everything in the name of the Lord Jesus [and in dependence on Him], giving thanks to God the Father through Him

Did you see that? It says now you're dressed in a new wardrobe, and the Creator customizes every item of your new way of life with His label on it. All the old fashions are now obsolete. Are you starting to embrace and believe how loved you indeed are by your Heavenly Father? God chooses you and me; He picked out the wardrobe himself. Can you recognize how special you are to Him? He has clothed you and me with His compassion and His kindness. Will you let His word dwell in you richly? Will you allow His peace to saturate your very being? Will you align your actions, words, and deeds to His will?

Are you ready to praise, to dance and rejoice, for how could your countenance not be uplifted? How could you not be found in a state of perpetual joy? I just told you your Heavenly Father, the creator of the universe, has a new, custom wardrobe just for you. In our society, in this day and age, we often identify or judge one's status by the clothes that they wear. We place value on others based on our perception of what we believe quality is.

We are so proud when we wear the latest name brands and fashions, when we drive the best car and live in the prominent neighborhoods. We place higher value in those things than we do in spiritual things. But let us not forget the true value lies in our spiritual connection, in our relationship with Christ. Our lives, our priorities have gone askew. There is nothing wrong with the finer things of life. There is nothing wrong in the enjoyment of having them but the error often made is we replace Christ with garments and status of men.

In our journey of life, we have been given the red carpet to gratify our desires. And in this world, to walk the red carpet is an achievement. While promenading down, the question continuously heard is "Who are you wearing?" because everyone wants to know who designed the garments being worn.

Galatians 3:26-27 tells us For you [who are born-again have been reborn from above—spiritually transformed, renewed, sanctified and] are all children of God [set apart for His purpose with full rights and privileges] through faith in Christ Jesus. ²⁷ For all of you who were baptized into Christ [into a spiritual union with the Christ, the Anointed] have clothed yourselves with Christ [that is, you have taken on His characteristics and values].

So, who are you wearing? Not what are you wearing, but who? Are you clothed with Christ? Is the status that you created your golden ticket? Is the label or the tag on your wardrobe lettered in gold with the initials JC or Armani? I'm not talking about physical clothes. I'm asking you to reflect on your spiritual priorities. Being clothed with Christ emphasizes whose we are, who we belong to.

To be clothed is to be transformed, a joyous journey of renewal in mind, walking out this newfound life in obedience to His word by faith. We must put on Jesus daily, not just that one time when we made the declaration to follow Him, but as a daily celebration of our faith, not living mischievously.

The garment we wear coincides with our character. His character becomes our character: Holiness, Godliness, humility, and servanthood towards others. Do you trust in His word? Do you believe that the penalty He paid was enough to redeem you? Our character displays a reflection of our love for Him. I confess, I myself have not always reflected Him properly. It calls us to reflect on our spiritual identity and commitment to Christ.

Do you need to throw away your designer jeans, donate your Tori, your Coach, Burberry, or Louie? No, absolutely not! But if your identity is wrapped in names that cannot save, then there's some work ahead of us.

All mentioned above is a metaphor. What I'm talking about is spiritual. Who are you clothed with on the inside? Being clothed with Christ requires a union, joining together, and becoming One! No separation is to be seen regardless of what may come.

Is Jesus being seen in your life and my life? I'm sure His presence in your life and mine will outshine the Burberry coat we may be sporting. If anything, it will enhance us more. I don't know about you, but I'm ready to wear my dancing shoes. It's time to wear the red dress of victory, a reminder of the blood shed for me. Just remember the finer things in life are not the reflection you seek; it's reflecting the one who has you. If Jesus possesses our hearts, He also owns our stuff. If we can afford to go to Bloomingdale's, we can afford to invest in his kingdom. Ah, a cheerful giver – a true gem in the treasury of God, but we must honestly assess what we are giving and investing in.

Are you ready to worship him in the dance of your life to show your expression of love by praising Him for His goodness concerning you? Are you prepared to change the story you have been telling yourself?

Put the pen down! Stop writing your own script. It was already written long ago, at the beginning. It's time to connect to the spirit of God. It's time for the expression of His truth. It's time for you and him to be united; embrace that sweet fellowship.

During my reflection time, a song came to mind, featuring Natalie Grant "When God Made You." I know the lyrics are often sung for a wedding describing two souls becoming one, but the words are so fitting for the wedding of the bride [us] to the bridegroom [our savior, Jesus Christ]. The mystery is revealed when our heart and His become one. A love that lasts forever. A miracle, when God our Father sent the perfect one [Jesus Christ]. No longer asking the question why. Convinced because of the assurance now gained. His love is eternal, a love that lasts forever and brings us great comfort.

Of course, I am paraphrasing, for the lyrics are not as written above, but there is a part that I love. It says, "I wonder if He knew everything I would need because He made all of my dreams come true. When God made you, He must have been thinking about me."

I told you in previous pages that God the Father had you in mind when He made you a new wardrobe. He customized it specifically for you when He fashioned you. Colossians 3:10-17. So, in the lyrics, when it said, 'I wonder if He knew,' my answer is, how could He not know? When it said I wonder what God was thinking, guess what! He was thinking about you. We make things so complicated when, in fact, it's simple: believe. His desire is for you to always have His best. That's in everything. In love, in vocation and career and in purpose and destiny. His desire for you is His best. His plan is simple, just believe and you will have His best.

I loved that song. I thought it was so beautiful and captured the heart of what the two hearts desired to display at the most memorable moment of their life of love together. Now, imagine love displayed for God if we can feel that for one another. Just imagine the love He displayed towards us. His passion has no comparison; no written thing can match this truth. No matter how we attempt to capture it, even if we had 10,000 tongues like the songwriter Freda Battle eloquently stated, you still will be lost for words in praising Him.

This reminds me of Zephaniah 3:17 I like the Amplified where it said he will rejoice over you with joy he will be quiet in his love [making no mention of your past sin]. He will rejoice over you with shouts of joy. What a promise! What great comfort, words escape me. This is the joy of God's love, a love that surpasses all understanding and brings us great joy.

Zephaniah 3:17 The LORD your God is in your midst, A Warrior who saves. He will rejoice over you with joy; He will be quiet in His love [making no mention of your past sins], He will rejoice over you with shouts of joy.

1 John 3:1 See what an incredible quality of love the Father has shown to us, that we would [be permitted to] be named and called and counted the children of God! And so we are! For this reason the world does not know us, because it did not know Him

Who loves me like this? What manner of love is this that He who made us has generously lavished upon us that we should be called children of God? This quality of love cannot be measured, matched, compared, or contested. We are all searching for love, to belong, to be accepted, to be part of, to be seen and recognized, and to matter. The ultimate love is Jesus Christ. God's love is enough; the greatest love that sustains and remains the test of time.

That, my readers, is the power of the cross. It is the love that called us by name. The love that lifted us as He was lifted up. This love destroyed the chasing of performance-based love, the striving love, the love you so desperately wanted from others that so much time was spent trying to earn it. I am so full that my soul rejoices; as the pen flows, the Holy Spirit is ministering to me through song, prayer, and poetic utterance. I must rejoice with jubilant praise of his goodness.

All you have been told, all who said you would never amount to anything, the ones who told you God couldn't use you, the ones who judged you, disqualified you, forsaken, dismissed you, forgot you, left you behind, turned away from you, didn't choose you, rejected you, didn't believe in you, didn't fight for you, didn't see you, didn't value you, spoke evil against you, cursed you, shunned you, reviled you, used and abused you, exploited you, and persecuted you. I'm here to sound an alarm.

Every thought, every lie, every chain is eradicated, destroyed, and demolished in your mind; that fortified fortress is now crumbling down in Jesus Christ's name. Like the walls of Jericho, it is no longer there, for His word has set you free. You are loved, wanted, and accepted; you are unique, memorable, and His.

The lies that told you you're not enough as you are, that you must modify and change to become something other than His original intent and purpose, are demolished. The chains over you, your emotions, and your thoughts are cut, discarded, and broken. God's word of truth has set you free. No longer shall you assess your value by your standard. You shall now consider the truth spoken by your creator—who fashioned and made you know you better than you could ever know yourself. Your daddy and mommy issues will no longer hold you captive. Your mind is being made free from those thoughts of rejection. You are being made renewed in Jesus Christ's name. You were never abandoned; you were never deserted or cast off. You are found. You are loved. For your God knows the plan, had the plan all along.

Jeremiah 29:11 says For I know the plans and thoughts that I have for you,' says the LORD, 'plans for peace and well-being and not for disaster, to give you a future and a hope.

This passage reminds us of that promise. This truth still holds true today and has the power to transform. Do you believe it? I know it was promised to Israel, but we are also heirs to the promise. As children of Abraham, this is also our promise.

His amazing grace has set you free. Your Father stepped down from heaven and came upon the earth, seeking and saving what was lost: you and me. The God of the universe who spoke and said let there be light, and it was, is passionate about you and me and desires to have sweet fellowship with us. Experience His grace right now. Open your heart right now and let His love in. May it be a fresh experience for you at this very moment, and may you be changed by the gospel that saves you by accepting this great gift. The news of God's coming kingdom, Jesus Christ, His Son, draws near.

The one who fulfilled God's plan of salvation by atoning our sins through death on the cross so that we, His children, may believe and grab hold of this truth and respond through repentance. May this truth of the gospel bring freedom and that the shedding blood of God's son displayed in pure unconditional love is powerful enough to cleanse, save, and deliver. By your grace, this was established. May the reader recognize their need for you at this very moment.

Remember the definition of Grace: the unmerited gift of divine favor toward man. Grace is God's kindness that we don't deserve. We didn't earn it; it is a gift from God.

By now, you're probably saying to yourself that God loves me. I'm loved! But do you get it? Each time you read it; does it unravel you? Is another layer of your heart coming off? The repetition of this promise that I am loved is deliberate for all the lies you and I have taken into our souls that tainted and bound us; we need to hear it repeatedly until it becomes our truth. It's already the truth, but we must allow it to become our present reality. We must believe.

Selah Moment:
The song that came to my heart, He Knows My Name, by McRaes. Take a minute to listen to it before going further.

Prayer

Lord, my prayer for all my readers is that they would stop seeking, working, and trying to be something they are not. Let the chase be over. The love needed, that is free, is found in you. Please help them lift their eyes up today to shift the focus from self and others and look to you. Let the agape, unconditional love you give transform their mind, heart, and soul so that they will be full, content, and made whole. We no longer need acceptance from the world, which will never satisfy the void within us. Let all striving to be enough cease. Their souls have finally found rest, the treasure, the value, and the meaning of a life lived in your abundant love. Pour forth the Holy Spirit with great measure. Pour in all hearts your overflow of love that has no limitation, believes at all times, has hopes at all times, and never fails. Let this moment be a profound monumental stone in all hearts reading these words. May they receive the great deposit within their heart: your love, supernaturally! Let them feel it pouring in like a flood, sweeping away all that once hindered them from accepting it. Father, I thank you for doing it, for revealing yourself to your children that they now know without waiver or doubt with great assurance that they are loved, that they are your beloved children. In Jesus the Christ's name, I pray. Amen.

Personal Reflections:

A time to throw away stones and a time to gather stones: A time to embrace and a time to refrain from embracing Ecc 3:5

This season may appear paradoxical and complicated, but it is not. I dare to approach it in the light of personal reflection. I myself have been a victim of stone gathering and throwing. Stones represent harsh words, curse words, and mean words. I have been a victim as so-called loved ones hurled insults and judgments. Why? Because I was setting a boundary, choosing not to allow others' opinions of me to define me.

Like in the story of Goliath, when David took up the five stones and slayed the enemy of torment who was speaking and mocking, I, too, had moments in my life where I could relate.

I also understand the season of gathering stones. The monumental stones and recorded moments are evidence of what God has done in my life. I have also thrown stones at others due to my hurt and unmet expectations. I know too well the feeling of being victimized but also giving it back, as if the result brought effectiveness and change. All it did was make me angrier, bitter, and more isolated than I was before I threw them.

Stones can hurt, they can destroy but they can also protect. They can be used to defend or inflict great pain and harm. It's time to clear out and put away those harmful things that have brought detriment to your souls. Put the stones down, let go of your hurt, and stop making excuses for why you think it's okay to hurt others because you have been hurt. I learned the hard way that broken people break things. Trust me I had enough knots on my noggin as a reminder. I thank God that no concussion was suffered. But it's also crucial to recognize our hurt's impact on others and be responsible and empathetic in our healing journey.

In my misunderstanding and lack of wisdom I have lashed out and hurt and harmed the very people I claimed to love. I see now and understand how hurtful it was and my heart grieves of the pain that I caused along the way. Now that I am able to identify that in my hurt, I hurt, it's liberating, but it doesn't stop the enemy, the accuser of my soul, from reminding me. It doesn't stop my mind from rehashing, revisiting, or walking in condemnation and shame. But remember, we are not bound by these chains. We are free from condemnation and shame, empowered to walk in the light of healing and forgiveness.

Throw away the stones of paranoia. Cast off the stone of self-exaggeration, self-importance, pride, envy, comparison, jealousy, and stubbornness. Come out from under the stone of "everyone is out to get me, hurt me, betray me." See, these pieces of rock, whether thrown or carried, cause significant damage to the heart.

We throw stones and live in glass houses. Not too smart. What happens when it has the boomerang effect? Are we ready for ourselves to be shattered? I used my stones to barricade and build a defense wall around my heart. I promised myself that I would never let someone hurt me again. I stopped throwing them at people, so I thought, why not build a fortress so tall, vast, and strong that nothing can get in? But guess what? I also prevented myself from experiencing the love of my Heavenly Father.

I cried out to be loved and accepted and to feel a genuine and sincere embrace, but my wall hindered my experience with God. The battle belongs to the Lord. He will avenge. You no longer have to try to protect your heart; Jehovah Nissi, the Banner, Protector and Shield over you, can do a better job. It's time to scatter what you once collected. It's time to let it all go. You and I can never truly receive or experience God's abundant life and live in His Holy Spirit by faith if we have a massive bag of stones weighing us down. The records of wrongs hinder you from being forgiven, for our daddy said if you forgive those who have transgressed against you, hurt you, and harmed you, I will forgive. Do you see the contingency word if?

Matthew 6:14-15 says: For if you forgive others their trespasses [their reckless and willful sins], your heavenly Father will also forgive you. But if you do not forgive others [nurturing your hurt and anger with the result that it interferes with your relationship with God], then your Father will not forgive your trespasses.

Definition of If: it is a conditional clause on the condition.

Note: *Forgiving doesn't necessarily mean regaining access. Letting go of the offenses in our hearts frees us. Forgiving the individual in your heart frees you.*

Remember that what Jesus did on the cross has the power to save and deliver all aspects of our lives. We no longer have the right to be the way we are when He made a new way for us. Your way, my way doesn't work. Discard the stony heart; let Him give you a heart of flesh.

Ezekiel 36:26 says Moreover, I will give you a new heart and put a new spirit within you, and I will remove the heart of stone from your flesh and give you a heart of flesh.

Hosea 10:12 The New King James version says: Sow for yourselves righteousness; Reap in mercy; Break up your fallow ground, For it is time to seek the Lord, Till He comes and rains righteousness on you.

Definition of Fallow: ground that is uncultivated and left idle.

The unresolved issues, unhealed hurts and memories, unmet needs and expectations, it's time to break it all up. See what happens when your emotions, my emotions, and thoughts are left idle? We become a hot mess. He can do what we attempt to do in our strength that has not worked thus far once we give Him access to our hearts. Stop keeping Him at bay, for He knows everything anyway. Do you think He is shocked by what He shall find? He knows you and I; nothing is hidden from Him. We might be in denial or have convinced ourselves of a lie to feel better, but the truth of our hearts is known to our Heavenly Father. Thank God for Jesus Christ.

God wants to bless you, but first, you must empty the bag and be free. How can you have a mountaintop experience carrying such a heavy bag of stones? The weight makes the journey longer and more arduous. Each stone gathered has a name or a cause, and it's time to let it go; let the pain go.

Jeremiah 17:9-10 tells us: "The heart is deceitful above all things And it is [a]extremely sick; Who can understand it fully and know its secret motives? "I, the LORD, search and examine the mind, I test the heart, To give to each man according to his ways, According to the results of his deeds.

God tells us our heart is deceitful above all things and desperately wicked. Who can know it? Does that sound like He doesn't know? And He searches the heart. Who is doing the searching, the Lord? So, when the Holy Spirit brings the matter of the heart to your attention, don't grieve him; don't pretend it's someone else's issue. He knows all that is in there. He knows every thought, every hidden sin. Nothing, and I do mean nothing, is hidden from Him.

By now, don't you understand that you and I did not have the ability, rank, jurisdiction, or authority to save ourselves? One higher, grander, more powerful trumped the ruler of self, and the government of the kingdom of darkness came and got us.

Only He had the authority. Only He could supersede the enemy of our soul because His kingdom is and always will be the highest, greatest, most powerful kingdom ever. Whatever King you may know, He is the King of Kings. Whatever Lord you may have read about, He is the Lord of Lords. The Kingdom of Heaven is it.

The season of resisting God's perfect will is over. Stop fighting the losing battle. Stop keeping people at arm's length; because daddy left you as a little girl, you are not open to being loved to let people in. Because mommy was not affectionate, that gives you clearance to close yourself off and deny the love that would free you. When the Devil comes to accuse you or your thoughts attempt to betray you, remind both of them of God's word.

Define domain: an area of territory owned or controlled by a ruler or government.

Colossians 1:13 For He has rescued us and has drawn us to Himself from the dominion of darkness, and has transferred us to the kingdom of His beloved Son

The territory of our heart and mind was once controlled by an unmerciful ruler: us! We were governed by the devil, but our Heavenly Father came and rescued us. He moved us from where we needed to be, the place we were meant to be all along, right by God's side.

Selah Moment:

What season are you in now?

Are you collecting the data?

Are you reminiscing of all the wrongs others have done to you, keeping a record of wrongs?

Is the word spoken forth setting you free?

Are you willing to allow his word to bring forth the freedom needed now?

Will you bring Him in to heal the brokenhearted and bind the wounds?

Are you ready to cast the heavy burden to surrender to him this heavy yoke?

John 8:36 says, So if the son makes you free you are unquestionably free

Definition of Free: not under control or in the power of another, able to act as one wishes

It's time to scatter the stone of offense. If you and I genuinely desire to be free from the mindset that has enslaved us, we can be free. The choice is ours! The stone of excuses for staying stuck is now demolished.

If you believe by faith that you are free, take God at His word, literally, and you will be free. You must walk this walk by faith. For you and I are crucified with Christ; we no longer live.

Galatians 2:20 I have been crucified with Christ [that is, in Him I have shared His crucifixion]; it is no longer I who live, but Christ lives in me. The life I now live in the body I live by faith [by adhering to, relying on, and completely trusting] in the Son of God, who loved me and gave Himself up for me.

Will you choose to rely on, trust, yield, and obey?

We were talking about stones, so let us continue. This season is a rocky one, so no pun is intended. A little humor along the way is a great aid when taking medicine that doesn't taste good but is good for us. We humans try to bypass that portion very often. We like sweet stuff that goes down smoothly and entices our pallets, but, for the most part, it has no health value, only to raise our sugar levels. Why do we take it?

I'm glad you asked. We want to believe we are doing something to get better. We convince ourselves that we can help God with the plan and assist Him in our well-being.

When we realize that we are still sick and all that we have done has failed, we've exhausted our finances. Then and only then do we cry out to the greatest physician, ask for a consultation, willingly take His advice, and try the remedy to be made whole, to be cured.

Meanwhile, years have passed. The initial remedy that God would have prescribed would have been two tablespoons of his elixir, but unfortunately, now that we are on the 7th or 14th of the 20th year, surgery is required. The quick fix is not the prescription needed anymore. God our Father is the only one who sees. He has the instrument that looks beyond the surface. He can go deeper than a panoramic view.

Definition of Panoramic: a view as of a landscape which is extensive unbroken and in all directions.

In dentistry, panoramic X-rays are two-dimensional X-rays that can examine and capture the entire mouth in a single image, including teeth, upper and lower jaws, and surrounding structures and tissue.

Now, if we who are limited can create something that gives us a deeper range to see further than the naked eye, then what about God, the one who created us and gave us the ability to create? Our view will always have limits; His view is unlimited, for our Heavenly Father is omniscient and omnipresent.

Definition of Omniscient: knowing everything, having infinite awareness, understanding, and insight. Infinite means limitless or endless in space, extent, or size, and it is possible to measure

Definition of Omnipresent widely or constantly encountered widespread something that is present everywhere at the same time the power of God.

You may be wondering why all the definitions. Well, I'll tell you why. As a visual learner, seeing helps me grasp and understand. I don't want to put big words on the page to sound or appear intelligent; that is not this message's purpose or focus. Understanding far outweighs big words, for the depth of sight matters most, and I feel strongly about that.

Definition of Depth: the distance from the top or surface to the bottom of something, quality of being intense or extreme.

So now that we are on the same page and beginning to gain some confidence in who He is, there's no reason to fear, for to know Him, to have Him, to believe in Him, and to love Him is the ultimate completeness needed. Nothing else can satisfy; nothing seen or unseen is more significant—the greatest reward to be achieved and ever gained, accomplished: our Heavenly Father.

Peel away the veil of deception, God! As the deep calls out to the deep, choose to see, agree with His findings, and be set free. When God reveals it, rejoice! Because the purpose of Him bringing it to the light is to set you free.

Stop believing the lie. He knew it was there. You and I sometimes don't know, we don't see, we're blind to His truth, so He sheds light upon it for our good because it cannot remain. Christ cannot be in us if we choose to stay false. Embrace His truth and feel the empowerment it brings.

We are to be purified by His word; let the facade go. I beseech you; this is an encouragement, not judgment. His love has broken every chain. We are no longer bound. Those who accepted Him and believe our wings are not clipped. So exercise your authority; it's time to soar like an eagle, take the sword of the spirit, His word, and cut off all that once hindered. Open your heart and embrace. Let this be the season of opened hearts.

Revelation is never for condemnation. It's for liberation and freedom.

Personal Reflections:

A time to search and a time to give up as lost; A time to keep and a time to throw away Ecc 3:6

The time to seek and search out the matter is always before us. Letting go of the past, which is lost, and looking towards the future. Throwing away can be difficult as we become emotional hoarders. We tend to keep the things within, that clutter our emotions. But when we release these burdens, we create space for the new that God wants to give us. We can breathe easier, free from the pain, the fear of loving again, and the things we know are killing us.

See, I know only one thing: I no longer want to be surfaced. It's time to get to the nitty-gritty. We have not and usually do not willingly excavate. It's time to go deeper than ever. We are here to find the buried remains. With the guidance of the Holy Spirit, this procedure is performed with precision and care. It's done systematically, step by step, ensuring nothing is missed. God doesn't want to dig a hole; His purpose of shining light is to expose, reveal, extract what was buried and cauterize, cleanse, and heal the wounds of the past. All this is done with the utmost attention to detail, for He is not in the business of harming but healing.

The harm done was by self as well as others. He sees it, knows it, and desires to bring light to it so you and I can be healed to make us whole, but here's the clincher. We have convinced ourselves that we are just fine. What does that mean?

I spent some time considering what that statement meant. How often have I heard it and used it? When I really could not put into words what I was feeling, it was safer, so I thought to say, I'm FINE, I'm doing WELL, or my favorite, I'm GOOD.

Fine
F ouled up
I nsecure
N eurotic
E motional

Or that all is WELL
W eary
E mpty
L acking
L ove

Or that I'm GOOD
G etting
O ver
O ther's
D isappointment

I've created these acronyms to define the inner turmoil that touches the surface of the emotions brewing below.

But am I fine, well, or good? Are you? We may fool everyone else, even ourselves, but we can't fool God because He sees beyond the panoramic view. Remember, he sees beyond 3D. He sees the core of your being. God is spirit, so what is unseen by the naked eye is seen by Him. That is why I asked you again what season you are currently in.

Selah Moment:
Are you ready to cast away the stone of self-deception and denial?

Are you ready and willing to put those stones down and sit at His feet?

Are you open to conversing with the most excellent therapist there is?

Are you ready for open heart surgery or even a heart transplant?

Are you prepared for brain surgery?

Remember, what we think, we become, and what we feel, we act upon.

The mind and heart are the two aspects of your body where He desires to concentrate. If He can excavate, remove, pluck out, and demolish what is buried in those two areas, the heart and mind, then the rest of the body will become whole, healed, and restored in time.

You are no longer taking the wrong medicine for your ailments. Without a proper diagnosis, how do you know what you need, let alone what works? Stop self-diagnosing. You do not have the blueprint on you. You did not create yourself. You may have made your persona, your false self, your doppelganger, but all those things, the apparitions, are not the real you; they are not you, not your true self. Your true self was created in God's image. His image, so He alone knows what that should be. It's not your image. He is trying to restore it; it is His image in you.

But what have we done? We've given ourselves a PhD in science and placed the title of MD after our name. We are our psychiatrists, and we specialize in our self-diagnosis and treatment for our mental brokenness. We have determined within ourselves that "I can fix me." What's broken is in my power to repair, to self-heal. All that happens without consulting with the Creator, with no blueprint of the original design on how it is supposed to look or function, so guess what happens?

We make frail attempts in our wisdom to put ourselves together without all the parts, and sometimes, it looks like we did a pretty good job. It sometimes looks fantastic on the outside. Compliments fly our way as our ego is stroked. Yes, we say I did this. I did it my way. Look at me, look at me!

Meanwhile, since we cannot predict the weather of our lives, a storm comes, a humongous tsunami strikes when we least expect it, and all that time, all those years, all of our hopes and dreams, all of our investment in self come crashing down.

When we put ourselves together, our stability and strength don't come from what we have built. Our ability to withstand to be courageous and strong doesn't come from us. All were washed away because some key pieces were missing. The storms of life took care of that: dreams shattered, death of a loved one, jobless, alone, and sick in body and soul. So, what is left is only our image.

So what did we miss? What did we leave behind? What did we discard in making ourselves our way? Our Creator, our Heavenly Father! I keep reiterating this point, and it will continue throughout each chapter. You and I were made in His image!

Selah Moment:

Are you ready to begin again, to repair what was broken?

Are you ready to start over to rebuild?

Are you ready to let some things die so you can give birth to your original purpose potential and walk in your true identity?

Are you ready to stop mourning and live again? Laugh again? Dance again?

Are you ready to lay down the stones of hurt, failure, and unworthiness?

Are you ready to tear down the barricades, the barriers you placed around your heart and mind, the ones you decided to build with the leftover stones you had?

Are you ready to weed out and pluck out what's choking your joy, hope, and faith?

This could mean identifying negative thought patterns, toxic relationships, or harmful habits and actively working to remove them from your life. If the answer is yes, then let us begin again. Let us rebuild, but this time, let us make Jesus Christ the foundation. As He is laid and firmly fixed in us by faith, we are assured of future storms, calamities, death, pain, heartache, and unforeseen surprises. This means we trust His teachings, love, and promises to guide us through life's challenges.

As we embark and endeavor on this journey with our savior, one thing is sure: this time, we are not building alone. This time, we have the most excellent helper, the best comforter, the friend that never leaves, the love that has no conditions and loves at all times, the balm that always heals, the advocate that fights our case, the judge that trumps all accusations, the doctor that has the correct diagnosis. The surgeon who knows exactly what needs to be uprooted, the teacher who leads us to the greatest truth to be discovered. The Shepherd that leads and guides us on His path of righteousness. The light that shines in our darkness so we may see and not stumble. Our Heavenly Father, our creator, our friend, our most excellent comfort, our peace, our hope, and the lover of our soul.

If you want to know why nothing has worked, why, in all your accomplishments, the void you tried to fill still leaves you empty, and how, in all the riches you've attained, all the stuff you've accumulated, you are still unhappy, and you do not understand why? In everyone's eyes, including your own, you have it going on; you are on the Mountaintop. You have arrived! You made it singing the song "I did it my way," yet when all is made still when the noise dissipates, and all you surrounded yourself with to make you happy, to make you whole, did not satisfy.

When the alcohol couldn't take away the pain, when the drugs only gave you a quick fix, a temporary high, an illusion of relief, when all it did was camouflage, when the lover in your bed couldn't remove the stain in your soul, or the marriage you believed would fix what was broken in you, and yet here you are, lonelier than when you first started, more rejected by your thoughts, more ashamed, more broken, a hot mess in the midst of it all, you remember. The word hidden in your heart starts to rise.

Ecclesiastes 2:15-16, 18 says: Then I said to myself, "As it happens to the fool, so death will also happen to me. What use is it then for me to be extremely wise?" Then I said in my heart, "This too is vanity (meaningless)." For there is no [more] lasting remembrance of the wise man than of the fool, since in the days to come all will be long forgotten. And how does the wise man die? Even as the fool! So I hated all the fruit (gain) of my labor for which I had labored under the sun, because I must leave it to the man who will succeed me.

Verse 26 says: For to the person who pleases Him God gives wisdom, knowledge, and joy; but to the sinner He gives the work of gathering and collecting so that he may give to one who pleases God. This too is vanity and chasing after the wind.

For those who don't know, this is King Solomon speaking. Rich and gifted with wisdom, he did not deny himself anything. Solomon enjoyed the pleasures he created with his hands and his wealth. He took delight in his work. He was rich, richer than most. He tried to cheer himself up with the intoxication of the world's offering [wine] as he embraced folly; he asked himself, what does pleasure accomplish?

When Solomon came to himself, he lamented. Why? Because in all that he was, all that he had and obtained, at the end of life, it was all futile; it left him empty and void. He is bringing attention to the missing piece of life, which is God. Without God, human wisdom is meaningless. Without God, there is no joy. We are stuck with only happiness. Happiness leaves us unfulfilled, for without God, nothing shall satisfy.

Our life is purposeful, and that purpose for which He created us is to know Him. How can you love what you do not know? How can you be like Him if you don't know His character, His nature? Who are you resembling? Him or a version of your creation of Him? Without the original blueprint, we cannot authenticate ourselves. Are we the real deal or the modified version?

Some artists have been able to produce frauds that look like the real, but regardless of how good the counterfeit looks, the original artist knows it's fake. For He who created stamped His seal on all His creation,

His name is on it, which authenticates who it belongs to.

The original design cannot be copied, duplicated, or replaced, regardless of any modifications we make. It remains beneath the surface. DNA serves as the blueprint of the original design, reflecting His image.

Divine
Nature
Authenticated

If you want to be the original, you have to go to the original one who originated you. You don't go to a chef to learn about the body. You go to a chef to learn how to cook. Stop looking to people, places, and ideologies that will never have the answer. All it can produce is a version, a fraud, a duplicate, but never the original.

Personal Reflections:

A time to tear apart and a time to sew together;
A time to keep silent and a time to speak. Ecc 3:7

Our creator alone is the answer, not has the answer, is the answer. That is why He came. Something got broken when Adam sinned. A tear in our fellowship, our relationship with our creator. Something in us was separated. Sin displaced us. The original design was tampered with, so God the Father, who created it, devised a plan to fix what was broken. To repair, replace, and return what was displaced [Him]. Jesus Christ mended what was broken. He authenticated the original design; that's what His blood on the cross did. That is what the sacrifice achieved, to make us whole again.

Romans 8:14 says for all who are allowing themselves to be led by the Spirit of God are the sons of God.

So what exactly did He repair? The spirit man! Remember I told you before that God is Spirit. What cannot be seen is more accurate than what can be seen. For the Spirit is eternal, flesh [body] is not. So, if we are created in His image, what exactly does that image entail? For what is His nature? Is it not Spirit?

The devil tricked us. He told Eve if you eat of this tree, you will be like God, but the Bible tells us that we were already created in His image. Displaced identity is a weapon in the hands of the devil and the battlefields of our minds. When you receive the truth, that is, not will be, not might be, your journey begins. The lie is exposed, and the striving stops.

All the energy wasted on creating yourself, your way shifts. You understand you don't have to recreate what has already been made. You decide to trust your life in the hands of the one who created, fashioned and knew you before birth. Your eyes become unveiled. You are no longer toiling, exhausting yourself, no more hamster wheel for you, because your Father creates you; you are His.

I know that God has given many the gift to see in deeper depth than I do, but as I am, He has chosen me for this task to explain His message this way. There are many books we can read that are wonderful tools of excavation. I desire that this will be one of them. A different tool is used for a different purpose. Depending on the job, some of us are plows, some are cranes, and some are rakes or picks. Sometimes, a sledgehammer is needed when the ground of our hearts is a little hard from years of unresolved pain and issues.

But whatever tool He chooses, each serves one purpose: to excavate, drill deep within, and aid in allowing the light of His word to penetrate the unseen, the hidden, and bring it to the surface. What interferes within us is the false narrative, not God's truth, which distorts who we are in Him.

Selah Moment:
Who are you?
Who does He say you are?

We understand that there is a season under Heaven for everything. We know life is a circle. Everything that has a beginning has an end, and when the curtain is about to close at the end of life, when we are translated from the earthly life to the spirit life, what shall we say then? For there is a life beyond this life. There is a dash in between a beginning and an end. The conversation we try to ignore, dismiss, or deny will happen. It is inevitable. What do we say then when we stand before our creator? What conversation do you believe it will be? Do you think your earthly profession as a lawyer can debate and win your case of life? No, not at all. The judge of all judges is before you. The one with all the evidence of the case of your life. The one that has the hidden camera you are not aware of. The one who has written every step you took in a log, what say you? Do you have an answer? Are you still convinced? Remember the song you sang. You did it your way. Is the blood on you? Do

124

you have the signed document that assures you of your rightful place at Heaven's Gate?

What insurance did you purchase? We, as humans, are efficient beings. Most of the time, we have enough sense and wisdom to put insurance on our stuff. If I have a car, I have insurance because if or when I get into an accident, I have the coverage and protection I would need if and when needed. Do I contact the insurance company every year and ask for my money back? Do I say, "See, I didn't get in an accident last year, so can I retrieve what I invested?" No, it doesn't work that way. You pay for the just-in-case, non-refundable insurance. You have that for almost everything: car, house, life after death, etc.

But what insurance do you and I have for the part of us we do not see? You know the soul part that will face the Holy Judge. That part we think we don't need right now? The part we sell to the one appearing as the highest bidder, the adversary of our souls, the devil. How amazing it is to me how wisdom of self confounds me. We don't see a use for it, but even the devil understands our worth, the value of what you and I are worth. He knows we are valuable.

The mind is the greatest battlefield of all. The place where all convictions and false truth and false identities begin. The place of reason, the place of intellect, the place where ideas are formed and then become. This great mind is the one that has excellent potential to create. Look what the mind has done thus far. Look how far we have evolved. We have credited this great mind to ourselves, but what mind should we have?

1Corinthians 2:16 for who has known the mind of the Lord so as to instruct him? But we have the mind of Christ. The Amplified version says, for who has known the mind and purposes of the Lord, so as to instruct him? But we have the mind of Christ [to be guided by his thoughts and purpose].

The mind originated in the beginning before the fall. The one we originally had when He said we were created in His image. The mind Jesus Christ came down for was to be restored. The spirit portion of ourselves. The mind of Christ. What the Spirit is can only be understood by the Spirit. The flesh nature is enmity to the spirit nature. The war we fight daily is constant and can only be won by the one who overcame and made us overcomers.

He promises us that we can do everything through Him, who strengthens us. All these things also include renewing our earthly mind and bringing it to the subjection of the Spirit mind in Christ. Our body is divided into three parts: body, soul, and Spirit. We focus on the body and soul for most of our earthly existence. In previous chapters, I told you about the soul and how it is our intellect, thought, mind, emotions, and will. Why? Because the mind is where knowledge comes from, yes!

Proverbs 2:10 says: For [skillful and godly] wisdom will enter your heart And knowledge will be pleasant to your soul.

Proverbs 16:9 A man's mind plans his way [as he journeys through life], But the LORD directs his steps and establishes them.

Proverbs 19:21 Many plans are in a man's mind, But it is the LORD'S purpose for him that will stand (be carried out).

1 Chronicle 22:19 Now set your heart and your soul to seek (inquire of, require as your vital necessity) the LORD your God. Arise and build the sanctuary of the LORD God, so that you may bring the ark of the covenant of the LORD and the holy articles and utensils of God into the house built for the Name (Presence) of the LORD."

These passages emphasize our soul's choice and refusal, which are decisions made from the will. They encourage us to set our hearts and souls to seek God the Creator. If we set out to do something, it is our will that carries it out.   Our will is the action part that carries out our feelings or thoughts.

The treasure chest is the place where our emotions are stored: love, anger, hatred, jealousy, envy, grief, and so on. All stones are within the chest, but not all are precious in His sight. The mind is the leader. The will has the power to control our actions and emotions.

If the will has the power, then why does the mind lead? Because what we think or believe we carry out. Your will submits to your thoughts and beliefs, then acts it out.

Your mind allows you to believe a thing; you give it permission to seep into your heart and convince yourself that your feelings are real; then what does your will do? It carries it out.

If I believe this is right for me based on my feelings, then why not? Isn't that how we guide our lives for the most part? But through the wisdom of life, we have concluded that not all things that feel good and gratify us are for our good. There is always a cause and effect in everything.

For instance, I can make a conscious decision that smoking is acceptable. I might convince myself that it's not harmful, that I enjoy it, and that it relaxes me. But the truth is, the manufacturer who created it knows the potential harm. They know the impact it can have on our organs, leading to diseases and even death. It's a choice I make, knowing the risks.

Alcohol, another example, causes liver disease, chronic diseases, and so on. It interferes with the brain, heart, and pancreas, but we still drink. Some more than others, and I'll leave it at that. All I'm trying to convey is that our mind is very well aware of some of the dangers we entertain and will still make the choice to engage in it because we tell ourselves it's okay.

We permit ourselves to do what we want. If you're a social drinker, there's no judgment here. I've indulged and partied with the best of them, too. But let's be honest: we must accept the consequences when our actions lead to adverse outcomes; it's our own decision. It's not the manufacturer who created it or the liquor store who sold it, but you and I. The power lies within us, with our will. We are in control of our lives, right? I'm using tangible examples to address a deeper problem: physical actions, but what about spiritual matters?

If what we partake in impacts our physical aspect, bringing forth evidence such as sickness, addiction, and so on, what is taking place in the spirit portion that we cannot see? Cause and effect touch all aspects of us, not just the parts we see. So what do we do about this will of ours, the part that controls our actions and behaviors and the part that tells us how to feel? Do we leave it unchecked to run amok? Do we let it go buck wild? Are we swinging our cowboy hats in the rodeo of life as the bull flings us all over? How long do you and I think the bull will allow us to ride its back?

Mark 14:36 He was saying, "[a]Abba, Father! All things are possible for You; take this cup [of judgment] away from Me; but not what I will, but what You will."

Jesus Christ's words in Mark 14:36, "Father, not my will, but thy will be done," Highlight the transformative power of surrender. He willingly surrendered control, relinquishing his leadership power, and submitted to the Creator. This act of humble acceptance of a higher authority is a powerful example for us. As the Son, he declared, "Not my will, but your will be done." Jesus did not allow His emotions, mind, or will to overpower Him. Instead, He chose to submit to the Father, and in doing so, gained the strength needed to overcome despair and fear.

In Luke 22:42 he said "Father, if You are willing, remove this cup [of divine wrath] from Me; yet not My will, but [always] Yours be done."

Christ chose to humble Himself, even unto the cross, for the sake of humanity. Everything He did was out of love for you and me, His creations. Like a proud father, He looked upon His creation and said, "It was good."

"It was not judgment that led Him to the cross; it was love. He understood what was missing, what was needed, and what was required for us to become what He originally designed. He is the missing piece. Please stop trying to fit a circle peg in a triangle hole; it will never fit! You would have to cut it down and reshape it to make it fit, which is what our will chooses to do. I will make it fit and still call it a triangle. Let's ponder this for a moment or two. Remember, all spoken words emphasize three things: God the creator, Jesus Christ the son, and you."

All examples are written to awaken the spiritual aspect we have ignored, pushed aside, denied, and overlooked. It is the part we have convinced our mind doesn't exist or is unnecessary, the part we don't believe is essential or required. If "I Did It My Way" is your favorite song, keep singing and enjoying it, but when you stand before the Great and Mighty King, a different song will be sung: "Holy, Holy, Holy is the Lord God Almighty, who was and is and is to come."

Romans 14:12 says. So then each of us will give an account of himself to God.

We will all stand before the Judgment of God and give an account. Romans 14:10-13 Out of profound love, not judgment, Jesus Christ came to provide us with the solution to our problem [sinful nature]. His love is a comforting reassurance in our journey of accountability.

Selah Moment:

So what do you think is at stake, eternal life?

Who are we accountable to now?

Who do we answer to for our choices and behaviors now?

Do we believe that anyone knows our deepest, darkest secrets?

*Isaiah 45:22-24 says Turn to me and be saved, all the ends of the earth; for I am God, and there is no other. **23** "I have sworn [an oath] by Myself, The word is gone out of my mouth in righteousness And shall not return, that to me every knee shall bow, every tongue shall swear [allegiance]. **24** "It shall be said of me, 'only in the LORD are righteousness and strength.' To Him people will come, and all who were angry at Him will be put to shame.*

The Creator of the universe is the only one with the right to ask you to explain yourself. He is the only one with the authority to question you and what you did with His creation because He created us, not ourselves. God created you and me for a reason. We are not a fluke or an afterthought. We were deliberately designed with purpose in mind. That day will come, and an account of how you and I fulfilled our purpose on earth must be given. Did we love him? Did we believe? Did we have faith? Did we trust? Did we obey? Were we authentic? Did we live for His glory or our own?

We have hope, which is trusting in the power that resides in the blood of Jesus Christ. None of us is saved by our deeds [accomplishments, works of the flesh]. Our works for Him are a confirmation that we belong to Him. Our works display a tapestry of love that brings glory to Him, who created us.

Our fruit is the evidence of our abiding. Jesus Christ became our Mercy seat. His blood became our righteousness, our covering, our golden ticket. We accept His mercy when we choose with our will and receive God's beautiful, extraordinary grace in Christ. We are rewarded not with judgment but acceptance and love as we are translated from darkness to light, receiving new birth as a child of God.

In previous pages, I gave tangible examples of choices that have a cause and effect that is detrimental to our natural body. The ramification of choices made brings forth evidence that cannot be ignored or denied. So what do we say about the spiritual aspect of self that we damage and bruise that we cannot see?

Don't you know that pain has an effect? The hidden emotional and psychological tares of life also have unwanted results. When you are born, are you entangled in bitterness and shame? Are you thinking to yourself at eight months old, how I'm not worthy, I'm so ugly? Why am I not beautiful like my cousin [Mary]? No. The love of their parents, or lack thereof, shapes a child born into this world.

Our environment plays a big part in our influence. Our parent's actions reinforce the belief system presented. It plays a role as we move from infancy to adulthood. When we grow and can make our own decisions, many factors introduced at an early age help influence what we tend to call that development. This vehicle is one of the tools we use to process actions: seen, done, felt, and heard. Effects on how we change and how we act determine the cause and why. Genes also play a role, so what am I trying to say?

Before we can make choices for ourselves, we have already been influenced in many ways. Our senses also play a big role in what we believe. We rely on how we feel and why we feel to answer the question of who we are or shall become. We allow our emotions to be the sail in our lives, guiding us. As the wind goes, so do we! Let's just go with the flow and see where it takes us—no plan, no direction.

Do you know why we need the Creator? Why it's so important to seek His guidance and wisdom to help us filter through His lens and not our own? Suggestions coming from the door are already altering our belief systems.

A lot of times, what happens to us has to do with what forms us. What we become. That is why psychologists are not surprised at all when abused victims become abusers, not a surprise. A child can grow up in a loving, supporting, caring home, and yet trauma introduced in that child's life can change the course of that child's psyche. Who can save us from this mess? It would appear hopeless, wouldn't it? No matter what I do, it matters not because I'm screwed. My sinful nature has it in for me before I can say Dada or Mama.

Here's the good news I've been trying to tell you. Jesus Christ is the answer; He is the solution, the cure. What contaminated your thought process, altered your emotions, and the foreign objects of sin added to your DNA have a founding cure. No longer do you have to accept the diagnosis given by man. No longer do you have to believe the report you convinced yourself about? You no longer have to look at your situations as hopeless with no cure. There is a cure—the love of God.

When accepted and received with your whole heart, it will transform and reshape how you view the world and yourself. The cancer of your soul doesn't need chemotherapy or radiation. It needs Jesus Christ.

The blindness that blocks your sight from seeing the truth needs Jesus. The portion of your mind that is handicapped by the idea of being made whole has a cure—it's Jesus. He is the remedy for a broken soul, mind, will, and emotions. Jesus can make all the aspects of your soul anew. He has the power to restore, the power to deliver, the power to heal, and the power to save.

The song that ministered to my heart during this portion of the journey was called Jesus Again, by Tamela Mann. Listen to it, I encourage you. Reflect on the lyrics for He alone can quench your thirst, He is the Living Water.

John 4:14 But whoever drinks the water that I give him will never be thirsty again. But the water that I give him will become in him a spring of water [satisfying his thirst for God] welling up [continually flowing, bubbling within him] to eternal life."

John 7:38 He who believes in Me [who adheres to, trusts in, and relies on Me], as the Scripture has said, 'From his innermost being will flow continually rivers of living water.'"

Revelation 21:6-8 And He said to me, "It is done. I am the Alpha and the Omega, the Beginning and the End. To the one who thirsts I will give [water] from the fountain of the water of life without cost. [7] [a] He who overcomes [the world by adhering faithfully to Christ Jesus as Lord and Savior] will inherit these things, and I will be his God and he will be My son. [8] But as for the cowards and unbelieving and abominable [who are devoid of character and personal integrity and practice or tolerate immorality], and murderers, and sorcerers [with intoxicating drugs], and idolaters and occultists [who practice and teach false religions], and all the liars [who knowingly deceive and twist truth], their part will be in the lake that blazes with fire and brimstone, which is the second death."

The Holy Book tells us that Jesus Christ is the spirit of prophecy. As the word of God, is He not the prophetic word that speaks over you, God's best, God's plan, God's solution, God's remedy? God's spoken word, so reliable and trustworthy, shall be fulfilled; if He speaks it, it will come to pass, for we know that God Himself stands over His word. He watches to make sure it performs.

Isaiah 55:11 So will My word be which goes out of My mouth; It will not return to Me void (useless, without result), Without accomplishing what I desire, And without succeeding in the matter for which I sent it.

Isaiah 40:8 The grass withers the flowers fade but the word of our God will stand forever

Why not place your trust in the one who keeps His word and has been proven and tried as faithful and true? His reliability is unmatched, and His promises are always fulfilled. If you believe it will work in your life, it will go forth and perform all it was sent to do. Will you make the choice today to believe? God is Almighty. You can place your assurance on Him. He keeps His word and does what He promised. He is the covenant-keeping God.

Romans 4:18 to 21 In hope against hope Abraham believed that he would become a Father of many nations, as he had been promised [by God]: "SO [numberless] shall your descendants be." 19 Without becoming weak in faith he considered his own body, now as good as dead [for producing children] since he was about a hundred years old, and [he considered] the deadness of Sarah's womb. 20 But he did not doubt or waver in unbelief concerning the promise of God, but he grew strong and empowered by faith, giving glory to God, 21 being fully convinced that God had the power to do what He had promised.

Are you ready to make the decision that will change your life forever for the good? Pursue your

Savior, look upon His eternal love, open your heart, and receive, for you are loved now and forever. Let the light of His love shine into your heart, for in His eyes, you are a precious jewel of value. God doesn't make junk. Are you persuaded yet? Are you ready to allow the brilliance of His glory to shine upon you so you may reflect His light?

Lay your troubles down, come and bask in his presence. Come and sit a while, drink him in draw from his love and thirst no more. We love because he first loved us first John 4:19

The blood of Jesus Christ, shed for us, is not just a symbol of forgiveness of sin, but a powerful force that reaches the highest mountain and the lowest valley. It will never lose its power. The lyrics, The Blood Will Never Lose Its Power, by Andre Crouch, beautifully capture this eternal truth.

Will you make the choice today? It's the best decision you will ever make. No longer weeping, no more searching or seeking, no more wandering like a nomad without a home. Come home, come to Jesus.

Come to the one who calls you His own. Come to your family, your true family. Let Him take off the filthy garments and place upon you a royal robe. Give Him the opportunity to lavish you with His love, mercy, and grace. Allow Him to favor you, to bless you, and to heal you. Accepting Jesus Christ will bring a transformation that will inspire hope in your heart.

With Him, you can cast away all fear. He will not disappoint, He will never abandon or harm, and He will never leave or forsake. Jesus, the author and perfecter of your faith. Jesus, the way maker. Jesus, the miracle worker. Jesus, the promise keeper, the light in the darkness. He alone makes the way clear. Listen to Way Maker by Sinach and feel the security and comfort that comes from His presence.

Are you ready to come to the one true God and not the one you and I have created? Not the God we created who loves us as we want Him to, but the God who loves us as we truly are in His eyes and through his heart. His creation, in which He was pleased when He created us.

I feel your pain, and I understand the struggle. In what my Father has given me to share, I will unravel the threads that hold the counterfeit masterpiece together in the upcoming Journey Of The Bride series. I will disentangle, separate, and peel off the next layer of the onion. But this is not that book. Look for future volumes soon to come.

This gem introduces the one who desires to commune with you in your new season. Remember I told you that you are partaking in the appetizer course? There are stages in our communion. As we build trust and intimacy, you will see more of me. But for now, my focus and only purpose is to unveil your eyes through the Holy Spirit so the foggy lenses can come off so you can see your Creator and, in turn, begin your journey of discovery to see your true self, the one He created you to be. There is so much to share, and so much to be revealed as each stroke of the pen guides me.

We were dead in our trespasses. He came to find us. He came to us, and we didn't seek Him, but He sought after us because of his great love. [Listen to Out Of His Great Love by The Martins] Feel the personal nature of His love, and know that you are valued and cherished.

Exaltation:

May the words penetrate the depth of your heart. May it unravel. May it unfold unto you the truth of the inner searching of your heart? May His love for you be seen! May it be so strong, so powerful that it shatters all the pain, skepticism, unmet dreams, and unbelief that once kept you at a distance.

May your heart cry out for the one that can save you. May your will surrender to the one that can heal. May this book be an open door to the great discovery of His great love.

May you receive and believe without question that you are beautifully and wonderfully made in His likeness, born with purpose, created with great design. May it be clear that He was thinking of you when He died on the cross. May His shed blood cleanse your soul.

May you receive His gift of grace as you journey with Him face to face. May your heart be open to His great miracle. Salvation for your soul that makes you whole. You're no longer bound; you're free to walk together hand in hand and never be left alone again. Jesus, Jesus!

The new song you sing, as your soul rejoices for the love in you, He brings. For you are His, you are free! At last, true liberty.

In the journey of spiritual growth and self-discovery, the light of God's love may shed the way as He grounds you in Faith.

My dear readers, I implore you to trust in the transformative power of God's word as you let go of the past, embrace vulnerability, and walk in the freedom and love He offers.

As you examine the season that you are in, let introspection bring forth freedom and truth. Let God's plan of liberation and healing in your current season open your heart to believe as the invitation before you is displayed. As you accept the invitation, transformation begins. Until next time, walk in the freedom in Christ provided by the cross of Calvary.

This is a final word of encouragement and a challenge to you, Beloved readers: have an honest conversation with God and undergo spiritual surgery. It's time. Jesus Christ is returning soon.

Selah Moment:

Do you know what season you are in?

Are you ready to release all the data you have collected?

Are you ready to let go of all records of wrongs?

Are you ready to scatter the stones of offense?

Do you understand that every situation is a time to ponder the season of life?

Do you understand that every situation requires every season to be considered and undergone?

Do you realize that you cannot get to the building portion until the tearing down takes place?

And you cannot get to the tearing down portion until the season of dying to the flesh and being born to the spirit takes place?

How amazing is our God to connect the dots through His word for us to follow; Oh, the excellent way!

Personal Reflections:

May these lyrics minister to your soul as they wash away every imagination, every lie, and unbelief. May the Almighty, great in power provider, banner, healer, sustainer, and deliverer, birth forth faith, confidence, and truth of His word over you. The Holy One, who sanctified you through the shed blood of His only begotten son, your peace, comfort, righteousness, and shepherd, who leads and guides you; the all-seeing God, all-knowing Father who secured your future, knows you by name. If that's not a reason to dance to rejoice, I don't know what is.

He Knows My Name – McRaes
Run to the Father – Cody Carnes
Thy Will Be Done – Hillary Scott
If Not for Grace – Calvin Nowell
Promises – Maverick City
Through It All – Andrae Crouch
Remembrance – Hillsong Worship
Goodness of God – CeCe Winan
10,000 Tongues – Freda Battle
None But Jesus – Hillsong United
What Love is This – Kari Jobe
Who Am I – Casting Crowns
You Say – Lauren Daigle
You Know Me – Steffany Gretzinger
I Am Yours - Lauren Daigle
When God Made You – Natalie Grant

Did you hear, **He Knows My Name!** I can **Run to the Father** and ask for **Thy Will Be Done** in my life. **If Not For Grace** I would not stand but your **Promises** are true. **Through It All** you bring to my **Remembrance** the **Goodness of God**. Even **10,000 Tongues** would not be enough to proclaim that indeed **None But Jesus** deserves all Glory, Honor and Praise. When I ask, **What Love Is This**? Or **Who Am I**? **You Say**, **You Know Me** and assure me that **I Am Yours And You Are Mine**.

What is your truth about **When God Made You?** Shall you agree and embrace the Father's heart that He Knows Your Name. Let your journey start there.

Epilogue

Seasons was an unexpected, yet very much needed portion of my spiritual journey with the Lord. As I was often hit with deep questions about my spiritual state, my inner parts were unraveled and exposed when the Lord asked What Season are you in?

I had to Selah in that moment. I began to think, but all I needed to do was turn to His word that aided me greatly in answering this question. I no longer had to struggle to come up with the answer, for He pointed me to the only answer, Him.

Imagine my surprise when He revealed that the only way to abundant life was through death. My death you see! How could I have missed that? Indeed, a time to be born, only came about in embracing the time to die. Yes, dying to all that I thought would be! As the tilling of the soil of my heart began.

Now if you know anything about a tiller, it is a pretty powerful tool used to break up the hard ground in preparation of planting more often than not grass. However, the tilling of the heart must be done with great care, so as not to destroy the tender vessels surrounding it, that brings nourishment to the rest of the body.

Oftentimes pummeling occurs turning the inner parts that don't belong to dust. Now I once thought the ashes were to remind me of the painful process that needed to be endured, however the ashes are the heap left behind to remind us of the victory as what did not belong was not going to go with us to the promised land.

When I finally let go of me and let God have his way, He proved that all things are possible with Him. His great love saturated my soul and brought me through the fire and the flood and placed me on the solid rock. I am not moved nor shaken for He has ensured the foundation that I am on now is Christ alone.

Continue this journey with me as we go through this seven-book series together. Be on the lookout for the next volume in Journey of the Bride Worshipping Through the Pain.

Take up the challenge to become the best you can be, ask yourself, what must I do to be saved?

What Must We Do To Be Saved?

Invitation of Salvation
Acts 2:37-41Amp

"**37** Now when they heard this, they were cut to the heart [with remorse and anxiety], and they said to Peter and the rest of the apostles, "Brothers, what are we to do?" **38** And Peter said to them, "Repent [change your old way of thinking, turn from your sinful ways, accept and follow Jesus as the Messiah] and be baptized, each of you, in the name of Jesus Christ because of the forgiveness of your sins; and you will receive the gift of the Holy Spirit. **39** For the promise [of the Holy Spirit] is for you and your children and for all who are far away [including the Gentiles], as many as the Lord our God calls to Himself." **40** And Peter solemnly testified and continued to admonish *and* urge them with many more words, saying, "Be saved from this crooked *and* unjust generation!" **41** So then, those who accepted his message were baptized; and on that day about 3,000 souls were added [to the body of believers]."

The Following Poems Were
Inspired By God
written by Kareen "FAITH" Casey

REASON FOR THE SEASON

In every season
there is a reason
under Heaven
God's purpose aligned
For all beneath his son has been
Allotted an appointed time
The time to plant, to weep or cry
The seasons of who, what and why's
The woven tapestry of life
The enemy plants tares to create strife.
But in His great love we
never escaped His divine sight.
A treasure hidden destiny within us lies.
Dormant and awaiting
His word of truth begins to do the shaking
We are rediscovered the great Awakening.
The gentle call beneath our true self lies
As it emerges a new season is at hand
Revelation given we now can comprehend
A time for birthing occurs as God's truth is planted
Destiny and purpose, are you ready to dance
Born Again, made anew His Divine Romance.

Kareen Casey
April 1, 2024

PEARLED CHAINS

Fear prevents you from moving forward
Anger keeps you stuck in your past
Deception blocks God's light in your heart, tares you
from him and keeps you apart
Dishonesty prevents you from growing
A veil of false beliefs that you can't or ever change
You lack confidence and shrink back
Never believing that you can be all that God
predestined for your life
Insecurity becomes your shield of faith.
Believing in the lies that you will remain the same
Unwilling to change what is at hand
Fear becomes your security blanket of shame
Your elaborate pearled chains
shackle your feet, heart and hands
You can't walk through it! You can't feel the pain!
You can't reach for it!
Stumbling again as you remain the same
You become deceived and lost in darkness
Creating a world of façade and sadness
Anxiety becomes your best friend.
Always there to lend a helping hand
Now trust is not in the picture at all.
The obstacles you keep clutched by your side
Prevents you from becoming His bride
You can't trust God! Can't trust yourself!

Can't trust change or anything else
The mirror you see dimmed by lack of faith
You see the pain, the dirt and only hate.
Your true worth does not unfold
You walk in loneliness never consoled
Inner beauty, what is that you say
How can you know if the
obstacles remain in the way?
So when God send his deliverance,
where is your assurance?
As you continue to pray, and stand in your own way.
Your shackled pearled chains are dragging your feet
Their names are fear, anger and self-deceit
Dishonesty, anxiety not far behind.
The lock of inadequacy bombards your mind
Remove the veil and stand in the light
Remove the shade that covers your sight.
You are wonderfully made! His words of promise
Let your inner beauty surface and gain your triumph
Free yourself! Let his love be extended
Only then can Christ's love be represented

Kareen Casey
March 13, 2001

SHATTERED

It only takes an instant to tarnish what God made clear
To tear down the bridges of the heart
that was built in a year

It only takes a moment to scar someone's heart
The words released without a thought
tares the inside apart

It only takes a second to shatter someone's dreams
Words of discouragement spoken,
and downright being mean

So please before you speak or act,
think on what to say
And if you are uncertain.
Get on your knees and pray.

Kareen Casey
July 13, 1999

CHILD OF PURPOSE AND DESTINY

Child of Purpose and Destiny
Remember always that I shall never despise a broken and contrite heart. Saturate your soul in my spirit and forever remain replenished and overflowing. See me in all your ways. Acknowledge my leading and be made amazed at my wonders concerning your life.

Child of Purpose and Destiny
Lay your burdens at my feet, in faith take big steps, bounds and leaps. Though many trials and pains will come, know that I am with thee and you shall overcome. Through many obstacles and oppositions, I have brought you through them all. With Daddy by your side, you shall never waiver nor fall, as you sojourn on to the call. A heart of flesh I give thee, Made pliable for my Glory

Child Purpose and Destiny
Never forget the invitation that you now accept. My bride in which I have entrusted a precious jewel to be kept. In you inscribed my living testimony the grace of God visibly seen, sanctified, made whole and redeemed.

Child Purpose and Destiny
Know that the seeds of calamity are crops of new victories in me. A vessel of honor carved by my hand. Refined in me perfect to stand. I shall pour forth my

grace immeasurably in thee, as you remain in the vine,
you remain in me

Child Purpose and Destiny
Know that whatsoever you sow in me you shall reap.
Therefore, strive to sow love, kindness, charity and
forgiveness. And you shall multiply within the fruits of
my righteousness. Be made filled by my Spirit. Embrace
my gentle grace, as I make your heart my secret place. A
gift of love for the world to see, Christ reflected in thee

Child of Purpose and Destiny
Be still and know me as your God, see me in all that you
do, as my spirit makes you anew. Let thy focus be on the
cross, as I send you forth to all those who are lost.
Remember my ways as my Spirit leads, Dispense and
also be made replenished and filled. Remember my
promises, which are true for you. Thy Heavenly Father
is Thy Shepherd, and I shall never leave you nor forsake
you. All that I have set ablaze for you shall be fulfilled
for I Am is the God of truth.

Child of Purpose and Destiny
Let Faith rise for the hour is now. Go forth throughout
the land and possess all given by my hands. For you are
destined for greatness.

Kareen Casey
May 5, 2007

Made in the USA
Columbia, SC
04 September 2024

41781675R00096